THE INVISIBLE HAND

THE INVISIBLE HAND

—

A Collection of Essays on the Economic Philosophy of Free Enterprise

Edited and with an introduction by

ADRIAN KLAASEN

GATEWAY EDITIONS

HENRY REGNERY COMPANY • CHICAGO

25106

As every individual . . . by directing that industry in such a manner as its produce may be of greatest value, intends only his own gain, he is in this as in many other cases led by an invisible hand to promote an end which was no part of his intention. . . . By pursuing his own interest he frequently promotes that of society more effectively than when he really intends to promote it.

ADAM SMITH, 1776

CONTENTS

MAN'S VIEW OF MAN
IN MODERN ECONOMICS
—
AN INTRODUCTORY ESSAY

ECONOMICS is the science that investigates the conditions and laws affecting the production, distribution and consumption of the material means of satisfying human desires. It is not part of the discipline to investigate the nature of man as he goes about his economic tasks. It does, however, require that assumptions be made regarding man's view of man before a rigorous investigation can be made of the processes by which the conflict of man's insatiable desires can be resolved in a world of limited means and resources. We shall therefore content ourselves with a discussion of the nature of the assumptions—both implicit and explicit—which are made by economic scholars as they attempt to solve economic problems.

The first abstraction with which we must contend is the concept of *homo oeconomicus,* economic man. We assume he exists. He exists wherever material welfare is regarded as sufficiently important to warrant sacrifice and effort. Where he does not exist, economics has no relevancy. It is conceivable that there are, or have been, cultures which were completely "other-world" oriented, but this extreme of self-denial is not typical of modern society. Regardless of how sentiment and emotionalism may deny the concept, human needs—from providing means for self-preservation at one end of the spectrum to providing material instruments and conditions for physical and mental welfare at the other—provide a powerful rationale for human behavior. This does not deny the existence of "noncommercial incentives," which are admittedly extremely important; it merely warns that a currently popular intellectual game has been made out of the fallacious interpretation of economic incentives as being non-economic.

We shall propose that four different attitudes regarding the nature of man are attributable to four different schools of economic thought. Recognizing that each of these schools of economic thought has been historically respected in varying degrees, and that they each contain variations accepted by modern economists, we can make the following proposition: Modern economics may be described as a weighted eclecticism: 50 percent Classical; 25 percent Marxian; 10 percent Institutional; and 15 percent Keynesian. The assumptions made in modern economics are therefore comprised of a conglomeration of the assumptions made by the authors of each of these diverse theories.

Let us examine each of these four ideologies to see what their creators assumed about the nature of man.

The classical position was most clearly stated by Adam Smith, although he gathered his ideas from a long list of intellectuals. The importance of private property as a motivating force came from Aristotle. The endorsement of work for the sake of making full use of one's talents and the condemnation of indiscriminate charity because it would lead to laziness came from Calvin and the Protestant ethic. The hedonistic philosophy, which interprets human behavior in terms of calculated comparisons of pain and pleasure, is associated with Jeremy Bentham. David Hume contributed the idea that there are four basic motives underlying economic activity, namely, the desires for pleasure, for action, for gain and for liveliness (as opposed to idleness). All of these ideas had one thing in common: they were preoccupied with the individual.

Smith's fame rests on his two important writings, *The Theory of Moral Sentiments* and *An Inquiry into the Nature and Causes of the Wealth of Nations*. In them he developed an elaborate and detailed application of the concept of a unified natural law to the economic world. The theme of these writings is that there is an inherent harmony in the order of nature whereby man, while following his own acquisitive interests and without necessarily intending it, serves the general interests of mankind.

The central thesis of Smith's *Wealth of Nations* is distilled in these paragraphs:

The natural effort which every man is continually making to better his own condition is a principle of preservation capable of preventing and correcting, in many respects, the bad effects of a political economy, in some degree both partial and oppressive. Such a political economy, though it no doubt retards more or less, is not always capable of stopping altogether the natural progress of a nation towards wealth and prosperity.[1]

In another passage:

> It is not from the benevolence of the butcher, the brewer or the baker, that we expect our dinner, but from their regard to their own interest. We address ourselves, not to their humanity, but to their self-love, and never talk to them of our own necessities, but of their advantages. Nobody but a beggar chooses to depend chiefly upon the benevolence of his fellow-citizens.[2]

It appears that Smith's contention of the existence of a natural harmony in the economic order is built up from detailed inference from the examination of specific problems and data. This inductive approach led Smith to the conclusion that man's self-interest is God's Providence. Self-interest to Smith meant not only the desire for worldly goods but self-love in all its possible manifestations.

What is man's view of man in Classical economics? In summary it is this: Man is an individual and is inclined to be competitive rather than cooperative. He is a hedonist whose moral duty is fulfilled in the gratification of pleasure-seeking instincts and dispositions. Man is good when he is ambitious and thrifty; bad when he is lazy and spendthrift. Man is acquisitive and susceptible to strong motivations by the attractions of ownership of private property. Above all else the Classicists believed that liberty and individual freedom were man's most priceless possessions. Man, therefore, is viewed as a creature who by nature resents coercion and is suspicious of a powerful state. And, finally, all these characteristics are God-given; they are part of the natural order of the universe.

We turn to the investigation of the assumptions regarding the nature of man underlying the second of our economic ideologies: Marxism. Marxism, which is often referred to as scientific

---

[1] Adam Smith, *Wealth of Nations* (New York: Everyman Paperbacks), II, 168.
[2] *Ibid.*, I, 13.

socialism, places the welfare of the group above the welfare of the individual. It replaces a competitive economy with a planned economy. Its concept of dialectical materialism envisages revolutionary changes in social institutions as a result of new types of man and new types of social action. Marxism proposes the replacement of the acquisitive society by the functional society, the rewards of success in the marketplace with the instinct of workmanship and the replacement of self-reliance and self-esteem by the spirit of public service.

Marx believed that the economic society which emerged from adherence to the Classical principles resulted in class hatred. Man's role in production was to some extent related to his ownership of property. From this, his social status, his aspirations, his mental outlook and his rewards differed from the non-property owner; the former became the exploiter and the latter the exploited. Because man's history had been a long sequence of class struggles resulting in social change, Marx predicted that the class struggle between the bourgeoisie (the owners of the capital goods used in production) and the proletariat (the laborers) would also finally end in a revolutionary reconstitution of society. This new society would be a stable, classless, equitable and generally acceptable form of economic organization.

A. A. Smirnov has described the essential contrast between the Classicists and the Marxists as follows:

In a capitalist society, the ruling class has pronounced individualistic strivings and interests. And so a decidedly individualistic psychology is typical of it. This psychology arises from economic conditions characterized by private property. The bourgeoisie tries to explain its individualistic and egotistic strivings as the unchangeable and basic qualities of human nature. But the only reason for this explanation is to justify the capitalistic order and to prove that this order corresponds to the allegedly innate egotistic strivings of man. Actually, the capitalistic order does not arise from these allegedly innate economic strivings of man. The real situation is rather the reverse: the individualistic psychology of man arises from the capitalistic order and wherever that order is liquidated, the egotistic strivings disappear in the end.

In a socialist society, the personal strivings of man are not opposed to the interests of society, but agree with them. Personal interests are therefore not repressed in such a society but, on the contrary, reach their full expression and development here, because they fully correspond to the interest of society.

Man is not characterized by the dominion of dark forces of the instincts or of the subconscious, but rather by the dominion of his reason which reflects the world clearly and correctly. We therefore consider the highest aim of education to be the development of consciousness. Instincts and the subconscious push man back, reason leads him forward. Whoever wants to fight for progressive ideas, for a bright future of mankind, must reject the theories which hold that the psychic foundation of man consists of instinctive, inborn or unconscious strivings. All attempts to uphold such theories and to justify the conditioning of man by instinctive and unconscious strivings, are in the service of reaction.[3]

What are the assumptions regarding the nature of man implicit in Marxism and the other forms of socialism? They may be summarized as follows: Man is a social creature and is amenable to placing the good of the group before his own personal welfare. The credo "from each according to his abilities; to each according to his needs" is consonant with human motivational behavior. Man's personality and motivations cannot be explained in terms of biological and natural drives; social influences embrace the entire personality of man and determine from the beginning his whole mental life. Individualist strivings, which the Classicists assume to be natural inborn drives, are viewed by Marxists as being formed by the influence of social conditions.

The third brand of economic theory germane to our discussion is Institutionalism. Its exponents in this country were Thorstein Veblen, J. C. Commons and Wesley Mitchell. An institution is defined as a pattern of inherited habits or a cluster of social usage. Contrary to the assumption made by the Classicists that human beings respond in a natural, basic manner common to all, the Institutionalists hold that man's actions and responses

[3] A. A. Smirnov, "The Development of Soviet Psychology," *Soviet Psychology: A Symposium* (New York: Philosophical Library, Inc., 1961), pp. 18–20.

are a function of his institutional environment. Original human nature is, therefore, transformed by attitudes engendered by the education, environment and institutions comprising society. Each society has its own ever-changing system of culture, folkways and morals. The compulsions determined by these institutions drive man to carry on his economic functions.

Veblen himself described the contrast between the Institutionalists and the Classicists in the following passage, in which rational economic motives are replaced by emotional economic motives.

The end of acquisition and accumulation is conventionally held to be the consumption of the goods accumulated whether it is consumption directly by the owner of the goods or by the household attached to him and for this purpose identified with him in theory. This is at least felt to be the economically legitimate end of acquisition, which alone it is incumbent on the theory to take account of. Such consumption may of course be conceived to serve the consumer's physical wants—his physical comfort—or his so-called higher wants—spiritual, aesthetic, intellectual, or what not; the latter class of wants being served indirectly by the expenditure of goods, after the fashion familiar to all economic readers.

But it is only when taken in a sense far removed from its naïve meaning that consumption of goods can be said to afford the incentive from which accumulation invariably proceeds. The motive that lies at the root of ownership is emulation; and the same motive of emulation continues active in the further development of the institution to which it has given rise and in the development of all those features of the social structure which this institution of ownership touches. The possession of wealth confers honor; it is an invidious distinction. Nothing equally cogent can be said for the consumption of goods, nor for any other conceivable incentive to acquisition, and especially not for any incentive to the accumulation of wealth.[4]

Institutionalism relies to a great extent on anthropological studies, and at times seems more relevant to sociology than to economics. It is, however, the basis for Veblen's explanation of "conspicuous consumption" and, more recently, Vance Packard's

---

[4] Thorstein Veblen, *The Theory of the Leisure Class* (New York: The New American Library of World Literature, Inc., 1954), p. 35.

"status seekers." The habits of consumption acquired in our institutional environment are not always rational and functional; they are often "wasteful and uneconomic" in the eyes of social critics. The economic problem of the world's producing enough for all is vastly complicated by the notion that our culture may have led us to a position in which we can only be satisfied when we can consume more conspicuously than our neighbors.

Obviously, the implications accepted by the Institutionalists concerning the nature of man are at odds with those of the Classicists as well as the Marxists. Man now becomes a creature of his institutional environment; rationality is replaced by mores; natural needs and wishes are replaced by needs and wishes which conform to the needs and wishes of his culture; these in turn will not have universality but will vary from culture to culture and from age to age. In contrast to Marx, who believed that the manner in which a society performed the economic function of production would determine the nature of its social arrangements, the Institutionalists believe that social arrangements and institutions will largely determine the nature of the economic structure. The whole concept of "economic man" is suspect to the Institutionalists. Instead, man is viewed as a social animal susceptible to scientific study. If man is acquisitive, his cultural environment has made him so. His individualism, self-reliance, ambition and even his pleasure-pain psychology are all induced by the compulsions of his institutions. They are not part of "human nature."

So far we have examined the Smithian, the Marxian and the Veblenese contributions to modern economic theory. The teachings of John Maynard Keynes, probably the most important contributor to economic theory of the twentieth century, remain to be studied. The perplexing problems brought about by recurring business cycles gave Keynes his chance to establish a name for himself. The Classical economists believed that in a market-directed economy booms and busts would be self-correcting, because competitive drives would force continuing marketplace adjustments directed toward full and effective use of resources. Marx, on the other hand, predicted that business cycles would inevitably become more and more disruptive as capitalistic exploitation of the working class intensified until, in a final disastrous depression, revolution would occur. The Institutionalists blamed business cycles on the fact that the important institutions were not well organized. The lack of a central plan or goal toward which all institutions might contribute led to a system of partial anarchy and this in turn created business cycles.

Keynes did not agree with Marx that the market-directed system of the Classicists would inevitably destroy itself. Nor did he have much sympathy for the Institutionalists' claim that cycles were inherent in the institutions operating in the market-directed system. Instead, he saw cause-and-effect relationships within the market-directed economic system which led him to propose compensatory adjustments within and consistent with the system. Group action was to play a key role. From his theories, modern economists have developed rules for the use of governmental fiscal policies to counteract business cycles and wipe out secular stagnation.

Did Keynes make any new assumptions regarding the nature of man? Probably not; he considered himself a defender of the market-directed system of capitalism, and by implication his view of man is consistent with that of the Classicists. In his early years, Keynes showed some disenchantment with Classical theory; he felt that the system in practice displayed weaknesses, which he attributed to faulty assumptions made by Smith and Bentham. In his *Essays in Persuasion* he wrote:

> Let us clear from the ground the metaphysical or general principles upon which, from time to time, *laissez-faire* has been founded. It is *not* true that individuals possess a prescriptive "natural liberty" in their economic activities. There is *no* "compact" conferring perpetual rights on those who Have or on those who Acquire. The world is *not* so governed from above that private and social interest always coincide. It is *not* so managed here below that in practice they coincide. It is *not* a correct deduction from the Principles of Economics that enlightened self-interest always operates in the public interest. Nor is it true that self-interest generally is enlightened; more often individuals acting separately to promote their own ends are too ignorant or too weak to attain even these. Experience does not show that individuals, when they make up a social unit are always less clear sighted than when they act separately.

We cannot, therefore, settle on abstract grounds, but must handle on its merits in detail, what Burke termed "one of the finest problems in legislation, namely, to determine what the State ought to take upon itself to direct by the public wisdom, and what it ought to leave, with as little interference as possible, to individual exertion." We have to discriminate between what Bentham, in his forgotten but useful nomenclature, used to term *Agenda* and *Non-Agenda*, and to do this without Bentham's prior presumption that interference is, at the same time, "generally needless" and "generally pernicious." [5]

This passage seems to deny the acceptance of Classical theory by Keynes. As he matured, however, he discovered, as many have since, that it is much easier to defame the principles laid down by Smith than to offer a better system. Although he recognized their weaknesses when writing his *General Theory,* he showed a strong adherence to Classical doctrines:

Our criticism of the accepted classical theory of economics has consisted not so much in finding logical flaws in its analysis as in pointing out that its tacit assumptions are seldom or never satisfied, with the result that it cannot solve the economic problems of the actual world. But if our central controls succeed in establishing an aggregate volume of output corresponding to full employment as nearly as is practicable, the classical theory comes into its own again from this point onwards.

If we suppose the volume of output to be given, i.e. to be determined by forces outside the classical scheme of thought, then there is no objection to be raised against the classical analysis of the manner in which private self-interest will determine what in particular is produced, in what proportion the factors of production will be combined to produce it and how the value of the final product will be distributed between them.[6]

Out of Keynesian economics has come, however, a rather complete preoccupation with employment, and the business cycle problem which gave rise to Keynesian theory has been modified

---

[5] John Maynard Keynes, *Essays in Persuasion* (New York: W. W. Norton & Co., Inc., 1963), pp. 312–13.
[6] John Maynard Keynes, *The General Theory of Employment, Interest, and Money* (New York: Harcourt, Brace and World, Inc., 1936), p. 378.

into one of employment and forced economic growth. When economists were able to announce the existence of the Keynesian tools with which the level of employment could be manipulated, the political scientists and sociologists saw in them powerful devices for accomplishing social objectives which were not necessarily economic. It might appear that Keynesian theory has shifted the emphasis from employment as a means to employment as an end. Remembering Frederic Bastiat's suggestion one hundred years ago that unemployment would disappear if everyone were forced to use dull tools, most economists still view employment as a means, the end being the satisfying of society's demands for more goods and services. We conclude that Keynesian economic theories have not altered the Classicists' basic assumptions of man, in spite of indications that some of Keynes' current disciples may see man predominantly as an employment statistic.

We have examined man's view of man as assumed by the Classicists, Marxists, Institutionalists and Keynesians. But in none of these do we find mentioned man's idealistic characteristics. What does the economist have to say about man's capacity for self-denial, brotherly love, concern for others? He can only point out that history is cluttered with examples of economic systems built on these Utopian ideals, all of which failed to meet the test of time. From the time of Plato's *Republic* to the present-day remnants of Michigan's House of David, man has sought to build an economic system on the basis of cooperation and love. Robert Owen's Villages of Cooperation failed. Claude de Saint-Simon's planned society failed. Charles Fourier's phalansteries, like the Trumbull Phalanx in Ohio and Oneida and Brook Farm in the East, are only memories. The search for Utopia continues, but the economist must conclude that the assumptions made by the Utopian socialists, e.g., that man is ruled by the heart rather than by the mind, are not valid in a society which is "this-world" oriented.

Economics as a science is amoral. It makes no judgments about what ought to be. Although some branches of economics exploring areas of labor and welfare are normative in nature, the great body of economic theory is limited to explaining economic phenomena on the basis of cause-and-effect relationships. Furthermore, the economist does not attempt to spell out which attributes of man are desirable and which should be condemned. Nor does he have any special competence in deciding what society ought to do. The social system will have to make judgments about the relative merits of individual liberty vis-à-vis a powerful state, equality of incomes vis-à-vis inequality of incomes, whether inflation is more desirable than unemployment and similar alternatives in the achievement of the economic goals of society. What these goals will be and the way they may best be reached will depend in the long run on the nature of man. The reason that different economic systems exist and that economists fail to agree on an explanation of them is that they cannot agree on the premises from which their investigations should start. They can only speculate on what will occur if their assumptions regarding the nature of man are valid.

The economists who support the Classical position have been reassured by the passage of time. Smith's writings were enthusiastically accepted when they first appeared in the 1770's. A century later a strong revival took place in the form of Neo-Classicism, in which the futility of social action versus market-directed action was acknowledged. Now, almost another century later, we again find a resurgence of interest in the Classical position and a revival of the so-called conservative position among young intellectuals. The underlying assumptions made by the Classicists and the reinforcing structure of Keynesianism can be summarized as follows: Man is by nature an individualist, created in the image of God, rational, hedonistic, competitive, acquisitive and imbued with a natural sense of freedom and an inherent fear of coercion.

The Institutionalists and Marxists, although not in complete agreement, deny the existence of a natural or God-directed order. Instead they posit man's evolution as a process of change brought about by his institutional environment. They contend, therefore, that the nature of man can be changed by changing his institutions through group action. Does the institution of private property make men greedy? Eliminate private property and men will share their goods happily. Do rewards determined by market criteria result in inequality of incomes? Replace the marketplace with the credo "from each according to his abilities; to each according to his needs," and incomes will be more equitable. Do market institutions induce man to spend his money foolishly? Replace market institutions with autonomous group decisions, which know better than the individual what is good for him, and he will spend his income wisely. In other words, Marxists and Institutionalists assume that man, knowing he is a product of his institutional environment, can reconstruct that environment through social action in such a way as to create an ideal man, freed from the crass and sinful characteristics created by his old environment.

Keynes said, "The *ideas* of economists and political philosophers . . . are the chief rulers of the world; . . . it is *ideas,* not vested interests, which are powerful for good or evil." Certainly modern civilization tends to place tremendous importance on the ideas of Adam Smith, Thomas Malthus, David Ricardo, Karl Marx, Friedrich Engels, Thorstein Veblen, Wesley Mitchell, Alfred Marshall and John Maynard Keynes. All the theories they espoused required making assumptions regarding the nature of man. The economic systems which will prevail will be those whose premises and assumptions turn out to have been most valid. Each of us will probably support that system whose assumptions regarding man's view of man most nearly conform to our own convictions. And our own convictions are probably influenced by the institutional arrangements which form our environment.

One thing is clear. The nature of man is an elusive abstraction. Not only are men born with widely different personality traits and into widely different environments; each man's nature is subject to fantastic changes during his own lifetime. A predisposition to a set of characteristics at one stage in his physical and mental development does not preclude the possibility of a quite different set of attitudes a few years later. This point has considerable relevancy for students of theology. In his *Goals of Economic Life,* Eduard Heimann, professor of economics in the New School for Social Research and former lecturer on Christian ethics at Union Theological Seminary, describes the basic conflict of our times as the conflict between two "rationalist systems," the individualist and the collectivist. While both these systems are "anti-Christian," he points out that rational individualism implies toleration, while collectivism repudiates it. Individualism does not inquire into motives but regards them as private and tolerates, among others, Christian motives. In contrast, a collectivist system treats the individual as a means, to be used or destroyed as expedience suggests, to an end—theoretical social perfection.

Perhaps the economic system that will ultimately prevail (and also the religious philosophy) will be that which best accommodates itself to a world in which man's most notable characteristics are his diversity and perversity.

ADRIAN KLAASEN

Part I

—

THE DANGERS OF ECONOMIC IGNORANCE

WE'RE FLUNKING
OUR ECONOMIC ABC'S

—

By Luther H. Hodges*

IF ignorance paid dividends, most Americans could make a fortune out of what they don't know about economics. Hardly one person in twenty has the sketchiest idea of how our economy functions. America may be the greatest industrial power on earth, but for all that most of us know, our greatness might depend on growing breadfruit trees.

Fifty years ago our ignorance might have been excusable. Today it is intolerable. Our country, locked in an economic showdown with world communism and exposed to intense competition from the galloping economies of Western Europe and Japan, is compelled at every turn to make economic decisions that are not only difficult but critical.

Wherever we look, some of the most important events are economic. All of us are affected by recessions, by unemployment, by inflation. As voting citizens we are nagged by economic questions: What should we do about tariffs and trade and aid to developing countries? How can we assure jobs for the millions of young Americans who will reach working age in this decade? Should we vote more money for schools?

Individuals have to answer these questions for themselves in a democracy; we don't want dictatorial men to make decisions for us. But how can we choose a course so the United States can grow and prosper if most of our people are, to put it bluntly, economic boobs?

---

* Luther Hodges, U.S. secretary of commerce from 1961 to 1964, received his A.B. degree from the University of North Carolina in 1919; he has since been granted honorary degrees from several universities. He was head of the textile division of OPA in 1944, and consultant to the secretary of agriculture in 1945. In 1950 he was in charge of the industry division of ECA in West Germany. Hodges served as lieutenant governor of North Carolina 1952–54 and as governor of that state from 1954–60.

The following article appeared in the March 10, 1962, issue of the *Saturday Evening Post*.

17

Consider just how unschooled we are today about economics:
No more than 10 to 15 percent of today's high-school students—tomorrow's citizens and voters—will ever take a separate
course in economics, either in high school or in college.

Of the fifty states, only sixteen require an elementary course
in economics to qualify for teaching high-school social studies—
the area where most students get their economics.

Surveys by the Opinion Research Corporation among college-
caliber high-school graduates show that only one-fourth realize
that the surest way to raise the standard of living is to produce
more goods per man-hour. Many think you can push up standards
simply by raising wages or increasing government spending.

This illiteracy causes us to choose paths that damage the nation. As an example, more than 16,000 businesses failed in the
United States last year. And why did they collapse? Mainly, the
surveys tell us, because of the economic inexperience of the owners and their failure to capitalize their businesses adequately.

Thousands of persons, with the happy intention of being their
own bosses, plunged into ventures with little objective knowledge of their market and competition. Some of these failures,
which destroyed savings and wasted national effort, could have
been avoided if the owners had understood simple economics.

Or take another example. America has for years had a favorable balance of trade. That is, we have sold more goods abroad
than we have bought from other nations. In 1961 the balance in
our favor was about $5,000,000,000, helping to offset the cost of
our military commitments abroad and our aid programs to the
developing nations. Last autumn, after one of my speeches, a
man came up to me and said that we would have to "cut off this
flood of foreign imports" to cure unemployment.

I asked him if he knew how much more we sold to overseas
countries than we bought from them. He didn't. I asked if he
knew that Japan, whose sales seemed to bother him most, shipped
$1,100,000,000 into U.S. trade channels in 1960 but bought
$1,300,000,000 worth of our goods. He didn't know that either.

Finally I asked how he thought we might continue to sell overseas, and provide jobs for millions of Americans in export manu-
facture, if we, in turn, didn't buy from other countries. Well, he
still thought the breaks weren't even and that "we have to do

something about these imports, or they're going to ruin us all."

Certainly there are cases where American business is being hurt by imports, and where some sort of government assistance is clearly justified. But if Americans form opinions about trade on the basis of isolated facts and emotions, how can we avoid making unwise decisions whose consequences may afflict us for years to come? Nothing could be more important today than a reasoned understanding by the American voter of the economics of world trade.

Economics teaches us that we must constantly choose between alternatives. No society has ever had enough resources to satisfy all its wants; we have to make the best use possible of our productive resources to satisfy our needs. If we spend, we can't save; if we buy this, we can't buy that; the more taxes we impose to pay for government services, the less money there is for private spending.

Economics offers a way of deciding the relative merits of this course or that. It insists that we define problems in terms of facts and identify our objectives in some order of priority. It tells us to examine alternative ways to achieve our objectives, and it gives us tools to measure the likely consequences of the various possible actions. In short, it equips us for orderly thinking about our resources.

All right, you say, but economics is a massive subject. A man can make a life's work of learning its tools and principles. How much economics does the average American need to know?

Last autumn a group of distinguished American economists and educators produced a report which answers this question realistically. The members of the group, the National Task Force on Economic Education, were appointed by the American Economic Association, and their study was financed by the Committee for Economic Development. The group meant its findings to guide high-school teachers, administrators and school boards. Not everyone will agree with everything the group said, or didn't say. But its definition of the minimum amount of economic understanding needed for good citizenship certainly applies to all Americans. Here, briefly, are the three main standards the task force set:

First, people should understand how a basically private economy fixes its priorities and uses its resources. They should be aware that it is largely the consumers' desires which determine what is produced in our society. They need to know how supply, demand and prices operate, why competition is essential in the market, how the government influences competition and the use of resources. They should recognize such basic economic concepts as labor productivity; the law of diminishing returns; saving, investment and capital formation; and the profit incentive. And they should realize how our economy is tied to the rest of the world.

I was shocked a short while ago to find that a college acquaintance did not know that the United States had a serious deficit in its international balance of payments. (In 1961 the deficit was approximately $2,500,000,000.)

Second, people should be aware that fostering stable economic growth and avoiding the peaks and troughs of booms and depressions is one of our greatest problems. People should know how we measure economic growth in terms of national production and income, and what constitutes a reasonable rate of growth. And everyone should be familiar with a few statistics and know how to tell, at a particular moment, whether our economy is doing poorly or well.

A short while ago, when I was in West Germany, I got into a conversation with a cab driver. I found he knew what the gross national product of West Germany was in the previous quarter and in the last year. I wonder how many Americans know what the G.N.P. was in the United States in 1961, or how fast our economy has been growing.

Finally, there is the question: Who gets the goods and services the economy turns out and in what share?

Americans should know that our high wages rest on the high productivity of labor and that inequalities continue to exist in the distribution of incomes. We should know, too, that profits come as payment for providing capital goods, taking risks and managing business operations; that without the profit incentive, we could not have had the economic growth that our society has enjoyed.

Certainly, the mastering of these few essentials should not be too difficult. The question then is: Where do we start to stamp out economic illiteracy? Obviously the first place is in the high school. We need to increase the amount of time given to economics in high school, and we need to improve the level of teaching ability. For years farsighted professional, civic, business and labor organizations have sought to encourage better economic education. We need more of this organized effort.

This is a cause in which everyone should be involved—as members of school boards, parent-teacher organizations, civic groups, as voting citizens. Only if you and I as responsible U.S. citizens work at this—give support to school officials who are trying to raise standards—are we likely to get improvement.

Beyond high school there are adult-education programs which can be improved to give heavier weight to economics; there can be more stress on economic fundamentals in service and women's club programs and in union and management education courses.

We can spread greater knowledge of economics through newspapers, magazines, radio and television. If many in this country read box scores about sporting events, might they not also read some form of box score that would give them information about economic events?

In the last few years we have mounted a massive offensive in this country to improve our standards of science education. I believe that we must now launch a similar assault in behalf of economic education. As Secretary of Commerce, the agency which is the nation's biggest storehouse of economic information, I intend this year to undertake a coordinated program, working with groups that have sought to improve economic education over the years and with businessmen, union leaders, economists and educators, to see how we can help get this mass assault started. You, in your communities, should try to get it started too. Perhaps you have some suggestions for us in Commerce.

Years ago someone said that economics was the science of stating the obvious in terms of the incomprehensible. Economics is not incomprehensible, as some schoolchildren know. And what it teaches is certainly not obvious, for otherwise there would be no problem of economic illiteracy. Americans can—and must—learn their economic ABC's, for at bottom the case for economics is the case for democracy itself—government by the people. If a democracy is to cope effectively with economic issues, the people must understand.

NATIONAL STRENGTH THROUGH ECONOMIC KNOWLEDGE

—

*By Adrian Klaasen**

MOST Americans would avow that they are opposed to communism; indeed, most Americans probably view communism as the greatest danger facing the United States today. One would expect this general recognition to have a unifying effect, binding all Americans against a common enemy. On the contrary, the specter of communism has had a strangely divisive effect on the American people and the schism created by our fears has weakened us.

One of the causes of the current divisiveness is a failure to agree upon the meaning of communism. If a consensus can be reached on this important definition we shall have made a substantial start toward reducing confusion. To illustrate how our national welfare and strength are related to economic knowledge, we will first describe the wide range of concepts which contemporary communism includes; second, define communism on the basis of its historical intent and purpose; and, third, interpret the implications of accepting the historical concept of communism.

Dean S. Barton Babbage recently gave a lecture entitled "The Disenchantment of the Intellectual with Marxism." [1] His point was that since Christianity had failed to solve many social problems, Marxism had had an early appeal to the intellectuals. This

* Adrian Klaasen is an associate professor of business and economics at Hope College, Holland, Michigan. He graduated from the School of Commerce and Administration of the University of Chicago in 1929 with a Ph.B. After a twenty-year career in business, he resumed his education, receiving an M.A. in 1957 and a Ph.D. in 1960 from Michigan State University. He is a member of the American Economic Association, the American Management Association and the American Marketing Association. Klaasen is the co-author of two books, in the fields of marketing and advertising.
[1] Dr. S. Barton Babbage, Dean of St. Paul's Cathedral, Melbourne, Australia. The colloquium referred to occurred during Dr. Babbage's term as a guest lecturer on "Studies in Christianity and Marxism" at Western Theological Seminary, Holland, Michigan.

22

appeal soon turned to disenchantment as the ruthless crushing of freedom and individuality turned out to be a price too high to pay for the promised social gains. Throughout the lecture the comparison of Marxism to Christianity persisted. In a discussion period following the lecture Dean Babbage was asked if he was treating Marxism as a religion. He replied that he was, and justified himself by quoting Tillich's definition of a religion. He described Marxism as a "secular religion."

One of Webster's definitions of religion supports Dean Babbage's position: any specific system of belief, worship or conduct, often involving a code of ethics and a philosophy. When viewed in this light, the Christian Church and Marxism are antithetical, and on this basis many religious leaders find grounds for an anti-communist position.

An editorial in the *Christian Century* of November 15, 1961, states:

> The conflict between Christianity and communism is deeper, more subtle, and more durable than the conflict between the United States and the Soviet Union.
>
> Marxism and Christianity are mutually contradictory systems of thought and patterns of life. Marxism calls for the substitution of atheistic creeds and secular rituals for the religious ones. Communism is a dangerous heresy.
>
> The conflict between Christianity and communism cannot and should not ever be compromised.

A second group of intellectuals, the political scientists, view communism quite differently. Their position can be summarized thus: The essential conflict is between communism and constitutional democracy. If we are to fight communism, we must:

(1) win other societies to democracy;
(2) work for better schools;
(3) work for better housing;
(4) win complete desegregation;
(5) elevate our second-class to first-class citizens;
(6) rejoice when our taxes are used to revitalize the economies of other lands.

Our children are taught to resist communism because political elections in communistic countries are fraudulent; because under communism political minorities are liquidated; and because democracy is the only system that guarantees political equality. One of the criteria we use in determining which of the nations of the world we will support is the degree to which their political institutions are democratic.

Dr. Sidney Hook, a leading American philosopher, in his book *Political Power and Personal Freedom,* insists that the primary issue in our opposition to communism is democracy versus totalitarianism, and that socialist economies and socialist planning are not of themselves an indication of communism. In fact, he bemoans the fact that some American opposition to communism comes from those who are against communism because they are against socialism.

We have illustrated two conflicting interpretations of communist ideology; this disagreement presents a first source of divisiveness. Christian theologians can defend their position against communism without having to make any reference to democracy, and political scientists can find nondemocratic enemies who may be consecrated Christians.

But this is only the beginning of the problem. The people whose responsibility it is to maintain a strong national defense program may interpret communism quite differently from the theologians and political scientists. For instance, Charles E. Bohlen, special assistant to the secretary of state, says, "The domestic threat of communism is *not* primarily political . . . but lies in the fields of espionage and infiltration. Communist ideology is not in my opinion among the controlling factors in its operation today. It is the *power* that constitutes the core of the menace we face. We cannot tolerate a Soviet superiority in military power." [2] Robert C. Hill, United States ambassador to Mexico, confirms this attitude: "If patriotism dies, so does the nation. We are in a great power struggle—our future survival depends upon winning this struggle." [3]

---

[2] From a speech by Charles E. Bohlen, special assistant to the secretary of state, reprinted in the Department of State *Bulletin,* Vol. XLIII, No. 1113 (October 24, 1960).
[3] *See* "World Power Alignment" reprinted in *Vital Speeches of the Day,* XVII, No. 5 (December 15, 1960), 137.

When communism is thus defined, our military leaders are compelled to respond by accepting the philosophy that the nation is best served by massive military might. The discord which arises as a consequence of differing interpretations between churchmen and political scientists now becomes more complex because of a third interpretation. To the militarists, all pacifists become suspect, including those who interpret communism as a theology or as a political system.

But even this is not the end. Toynbee represents a historian's viewpoint. To him communism is a system of darkness as opposed to light, a system of slavery as opposed to freedom.

> The cold war is a dispute in which the issues themselves are disputable. Each side claims to be the champion of light against darkness and often rejects the identical claim which the other side asserts. The reason is that socialism and free enterprise are two sides of an identical suit of clothes; namely, they both apply to economic systems. And when the standards of living between these giants shall have been equalized, the only remaining difference will be freedom —the economic problems are not worth arguing about—the only essential element of difference between capitalism and communism is spiritual freedom. In this respect they are opposite and irreconcilable.[4]

He asks which of the two power blocs will be able to give the lion's share of help to the underdeveloped countries of the world. The march of history will pass by the loser in this competition and leave it stranded. "Basically," says Toynbee, "the winner will be the system that creates the greatest social justice, and one way of achieving such justice is to transfer the purchasing power of Americans from needs they do not have to the needs that Asians, Africans and Latin Americans certainly do have." This reasoning leads Toynbee to the intemperate conclusion that Madison Avenue is a greater threat to America than communism.

Other fields of intellectual endeavor are equally productive of a proliferation of definitions.

Sociologists are often concerned with devising means for helping underdeveloped societies; the methods they propose are usu-

---

[4] From "Spiritual Freedom Is the Great Difference," the *New York Times Magazine,* January 15, 1961.

ally socialistic. One does not have to spend many hours with the *Annals* of the American Academy of Political and Social Science to observe that whenever a conflict is recognized between private and public action in meeting health needs, educational needs, international trade and cooperation it is usually resolved in favor of some sort of government action. They often find themselves hard-pressed to find a rationale for joining the popular anticommunist line. Their concept of communism, therefore, identifies self-interest with an attitude which aids and abets the communistic philosophy.

Labor leaders have still different notions of why they are opposed to communism:

> Communism in the public mind has become associated with subversion, aggression, brutality, slave labor, denial of civil liberties. These are the reasons for labor's opposition—and to generate fresh appeal among the working class the socialists therefore are faced with the necessity of divesting themselves from Marxism ideology and of devising a program based on the concept of the welfare state.[5]

It will come as a surprise to most people that none of the concepts described in the foregoing pages accurately describes communism. Webster defines communism as "an *economic* theory or system of the ownership of all property by the community as a whole; . . . theoretically based on the doctrines of Marx and Engels . . . characterized by state planning and control of the economy." [6]

Now the circle of confusion is complete. The religious intellectual may find the economics of communism acceptable, the politics acceptable, but Marxism as a religion, repugnant. The political scientist may find no fault with the economics of collectivism or with communism as a religion but abhors it as a political system. The greatest cause of divisiveness, however, stems from the total lack of realization on the part of the American people that economics is the most relevant concept in understanding communism.

---

[5] David J. Sapoff, "The Course of Ideology in International Labor," *Monthly Labor Review,* October, 1960, p. 1031.
[6] *Webster's New World Dictionary, College Edition* (Cleveland: The World Publishing Co., 1957).

Marx was primarily an economist. The greater part of his life was spent in economic study, and his writings, as exemplified by the monumental study *Das Kapital,* are studies of economic doctrine. The basis for communism is the *Communist Manifesto,* which Marx and Engels, another economist, collaborated to produce. It therefore seems reasonable to look to Marx and his writings if we are to arrive objectively at an intelligent definition of the nature of communism.

Marx's first and foremost principle was that the fundamental causes of men's actions and the social systems they create are economic; his concept of dialectical materialism stresses the claim that the material circumstances, material environment and the conditions surrounding the practical struggle of man to satisfy his daily wants and needs are the factors which determine the social system that shall prevail.

From this position Marxist dogma proceeds to trace the "inevitable" evolution of capitalism, which ultimately leads to its own destruction. The development of Marxian logic in predicting capitalism's self-destruction leans heavily on three hypotheses (although Marx does not recognize them as such): (1) Under capitalism there must be two opposing forces which are mutually incompatible—the proletariat, which consists of the workers, and the bourgeoisie, consisting of the owner-entrepreneurs; (2) The value of all goods depends upon the amount of labor required to produce them; (3) Capitalism must lead to imperialism.

Marx used a highly emotional attack on the institution of private property in developing the thesis that inevitably the worker would be driven into slavery and subsistence wages under capitalism. The rationale of this prediction was an invention of Thomas Malthus—that as a population prospered it would expand, and the resultant expansion would create an oversupply of labor. The oversupply of labor, in turn, would drive wages down until finally and inevitably all workers would be reduced to a bare subsistence level of existence. Marx proposed, therefore, to put all property in the hands of a centralized authority. This would automatically destroy capitalism.

Marx justified this expropriation of property on the grounds that only the worker could produce value and that members of the bourgeoisie were social leeches. Marx spent many years of his life in a futile effort to establish this specious claim. The complex and confusing arguments he used to establish the labor value theory are beyond the scope of this paper. His conclusion, however, was that the value of a commodity depended upon the amount of labor consumed in producing it. The labor need not be limited to direct labor; it included overhead and the labor which built the factory, the machines and everything that in any way contributed to the product. Again, this was not an original idea but was the expansion of a concept which David Ricardo had attempted to develop earlier. Even the notion that capitalism must engage in imperialistic exploitation if it is to survive was first developed by Hobson, and Marx merely embellished it.

Marx adroitly wove these three hypotheses into a prediction that a wave of booms and busts would be set in motion which would eventually lead to such extremes of unemployment and misery that the whole system would destroy itself and finally the expropriators would become the expropriated.

History has destroyed the validity of the three hypotheses upon which Marx built his dire predictions. Capitalism has not doomed the worker to an inevitable propertyless pauperism; it has provided instead a medium by which the nearest approach to a classless society has been achieved by permitting a high degree of interclass mobility. The labor theory of value has been discredited by most economists, and the contribution of capital and entrepreneurship is generally recognized. And, finally, Marx's association of expanding capitalism with imperialistic exploitation betrays his lack of appreciation of how the unfettered marketplace tends to correct each economic system's deficiencies through the operation of the price system. When an underdeveloped country desperately needs capital to improve its productivity, this need will be reflected in higher interest rates, which in turn will tend to attract the needed capital. To label this simple market phenomenon "capitalistic exploitation" as convincingly as Marx did constitutes one of his most ruthless hoaxes.

We have attempted to clarify the concept of communism by identifying Marx as an economist first; his prognosis of capitalism's self-destruction makes him a revolutionary only incidentally. We have reviewed his writings and have found them to be largely preoccupied with economic problems. We have seen his attempt to solve these problems by proposing an economic system which, he believed, would be more productive of total satisfactions than the present system of market-directed capitalism.

His ideas have been accepted largely as a result of their being promoted with missionary zeal by his followers. Whenever we have contrasted communism with Christianity, or communism with democracy, or communism with freedom and peace, we have revealed a preoccupation with Marx the revolutionary. But in the final analysis, it is Marx the economist with whom we must contend. The logic of Marx's dialectical materialism is impeccable. The culture of each society inevitably *does* reflect the arrangement under which that society produces the goods and services it needs and wants. It follows, therefore, that in our capitalistic society our present institutions, cultures and mores reflect the ideologies of capitalism, and if capitalism is to perish, a new environment will have to be accepted.

We can now make some useful deductions regarding the current problem of divisiveness. In the first place, communism must be treated as an *economic system* which is the antithesis of capitalism. Secondly, there is a strong implication that the survivor in the struggle between communism and capitalism will be that system which performs the *economic tasks* most efficiently and most nearly in conformity with society's economic goals. And, thirdly, if our intellectual and political leaders are to carry out their roles responsibly, they will have to acquire a degree of *economic literacy* beyond that exhibited by the majority of them today.

The problem of creating some degree of economic literacy among our leaders is not only of long standing, but is deeply rooted. The miracle of the market-directed economy—an economy which permits anyone in our society to acquire almost anything he needs in exchange for a few hours of his time—is taken for granted, and the usefulness of studying the complicated phenomenon involved never seems to occur to its beneficiaries.

We have shown how substantial segments of our society have interpreted communism to be an evil because of their egocentric views of communism. Theologians who define Marxism in terms of a religion, political scientists who view communism as a political system and militarists who view communism as a great power threat add to the confusion and divisiveness. If we can agree that communism is primarily an *economic* system, which threatens the existing order and incidentally poses these other threats, then we have a basis for joining all segments of our society into a unified resistance to the real threat which communism poses. To the extent that we can support private enterprise and defend it intelligently—at all intellectual levels—we shall have eliminated communism's most powerful weapon, our own divisiveness.

THE INTELLECTUAL
AND THE MARKETPLACE

—

By George J. Stigler*

THE intellectual has never felt kindly toward the marketplace: to him it has always been a place of vulgar men and of base motives. Whether this intellectual was an ancient Greek philosopher, who viewed economic life as an unpleasant necessity which should never be allowed to become obtrusive or dominant, or whether this intellectual is a modern man, who focuses his scorn on gadgets and Madison Avenue, the base similarity of view has been pronounced.

Now you and I are intellectuals, as this word is used. I am one automatically, because I am a professor and buy more books than golf clubs. You are intellectuals because you are drawn from the most intelligent tenth of the population, most of you will go on to graduate school and you would rather be a United States senator or a Nobel Laureate than the head of the Great Atlantic and Pacific Tea Company. The question I wish to pose is not whether we should love the marketplace—even a professor of economics of outrageously conservative tendencies cannot bring himself to say that the chants of five auctioneers rival a Mozart quintet. The questions are, rather: What don't we like about the marketplace; and, are we sure that our attitudes are socially useful?

* George J. Stigler is the Charles R. Walgreen professor of American institutions and director of the Walgreen Foundation at the University of Chicago's Graduate School of Business. Currently president of the American Economic Association, Stigler is a member of the American Philosophical Society, the Royal Economics Society and the Universities National Bureau Committee for Economic Research. A member of the research staff of the National Bureau of Economic Research since 1941, he was chairman of the price statistics review committee for that organization in 1960–61.

Stigler is the author of numerous articles on economics; his books include *The Theory of Price* (1946) and *Capital and Rates of Return in Manufacturing* (1963).

"The Intellectual and the Marketplace" was presented to a convocation of the student body at Carleton College, Northfield, Minnesota.

Let us begin by noticing that from certain important viewpoints one would have expected the intellectuals to be very kindly disposed toward that system of private enterprise which I call the marketplace.

First, if I may introduce a practical consideration, intellectuals by and large have elevated tastes—they like to eat, dress and live well, and especially to travel. The late Walton Hamilton, lawyer and economist, once said that our customary salutation "Good Day" was a vestige of an agricultural society where people were asking for good weather, and he expected city dwellers eventually to greet each other with the phrase "Low Prices." If Hamilton's theory is correct, the intellectuals will come to the salutation "Fair Fullbright."

Since intellectuals are not inexpensive, until the rise of the modern enterprise system no society could afford many intellectuals. As a wild guess, the full-time intellectuals numbered 200 in Athens in the extraordinary age of Pericles, or about one for every 1,500 of population. And at most times in later history the intellectuals fell far, far short of this proportion. Today there are at least 1,000,000 in the United States, taking only a fraction of those who live by pen and tongue into account, or one for each 200 of population. At least four out of every five of us owe our pleasant lives to the great achievements of the marketplace. We professors are much more beholden to Henry Ford than to the foundation which bears his name and spreads his assets.

Not only have the productive achievements of the marketplace supported a much-enlarged intellectual class, but also the leaders of the marketplace have personally been strong supporters of the intellectuals, and in particular those in the academic world. If one asks where, in the Western university world, the freedom of inquiry of professors has been most staunchly defended and energetically promoted, my answer is this: not in the politically controlled universities, whether in the United States or Germany —legislatures are not overpopulated with tolerant men indifferent to popularity. Not in the self-perpetuating faculties, such as Oxford and Cambridge from 1700 to 1850—even intellectuals can become convinced that they have acquired ultimate truth, and that it can be preserved indefinitely by airing it before students once a year. No, inquiry has been most free in the college whose trustees are a group of top quality leaders of the marketplace—men who, our experience shows, are remarkably tolerant of almost everything except a mediocre and complacent faculty. Economics provides many examples: If a professor wishes to denounce aspects of big business, as I have, he will be wise to locate in a school whose trustees are big businessmen, and I have.

But debts are seldom the basis for friendship, and there is a much more powerful reason the intellectual might be sympathetic to the marketplace: the organizing principles of both areas are the same.

An enterprise system is a system of voluntary contract. Neither fraud nor coercion is within the ethics of the market system. Indeed, there is no possibility of coercion in a pure enterprise system, because the competition of rivals provides alternatives to every buyer or seller. All real economic systems contain some monopoly, and hence some coercive power for particular individuals; but the amount and the extent of such monopoly power are usually much exaggerated, and in any case monopoly is not an integral part of the logic of the system.

The intellectual world, and I speak chiefly but not exclusively of scholarship, is also a voluntary system. Its central credo is that opinions are to be formed through free discussion on the basis of full disclosure of evidence. Fraud and coercion are equally repugnant to the scholar. The freedom of thought is preserved by the open competition of scholars and ideas. Authority, the equivalent of monopoly power, is the great enemy of freedom of inquiry. Competition in scholarship is in some ways more violent than in business: the law sets limits on the disparagement of a rival's product, unless it is done in a book review in a learned journal.

Just as real markets have some fraud and monopoly which impair the claims for the marketplace, so the intellectual world has its instances of coercion and deception, with the coercion exercised by claques and fashion. But again these deviants are outside the logic of the system.

Both areas, moreover, are democratic. The intellectual believes that every able and willing young person should get a good education, whatever his race or financial background. The market believes every able and willing person should be permitted to enter any industry or occupation, whatever his race or educational background. There is food for thought in the fact that racial discrimination has diminished earlier, faster and more quietly in the marketplace than in political life.

The analogies could be pursued much further, although not without danger of alienating all professors and most businessmen. I shall therefore merely mention, in passing, that both fields pay a fair amount of attention to packaging and advertising, and both fields place an absurdly high value on originality. There are also many minor differences, such as that the intellectual has no desire to know the marketplace, whereas the businessman wishes, or at least believes he wishes, to know the world of the intellectual. The basic fact is that the intellectual believes in the free market in ideas and, what is not quite the same thing, in words.

Yet whatever the latent sympathies of the intellectual for the marketplace, the hostilities are overt. The contempt for the "profit motive" which directs economic activity is widespread, and the suspicion of the behavior to which it leads is deep-seated. The charge that American society is materialistic has been recited more often than the Declaration of Independence and has been translated into more foreign languages.

In one basic respect I believe that the criticism by the intellectuals is misplaced, and at times even hypocritical. The American economy produces many goods that are vulgar, silly or meretricious, as judged by standards which I share with many intellectuals. It seems only proper to cite a few examples, if only to show how selective these standards are. I shall not propose the currently most popular item, the large and powerful automobile, because I have observed that mostly intellectuals of short stature criticize our cars. But other examples are at hand. I am dissatisfied with the tastes of the nine-tenths of the population which believes that nonfictional books are to be read only by young people working for their B.A. I am dissatisfied with a population whose love for interesting music is so narrow that every symphony orchestra requires subsidies. I consider it shocking that more Americans have read *The Affluent Society* than *The Wealth of Nations*.

At the risk of appearing reasonable, I wish to qualify this complaint by observing that the tastes of the American public are more elevated than those of any other large society in history. Most societies have been judged by their cultural aristocracies—indeed, in earlier periods the vast majority of the population was not even considered to be a part of the culture of the society, for this vast majority was illiterate, tradition-bound, with most people living brutishly in peasant huts. Our society's tastes are judged by those of the vast majority of the population, and this majority is generous, uncomplacent and hard-working, with unprecedentedly large numbers engaged in further self-education, or eagerly patronizing the arts. Our market-supported legitimate theater, which is surely the best in the world, is a suggestive measure of popular tastes.

These qualifications are not intended to withdraw the charge that the public's tastes should be better, and, for that matter, that the intellectual's tastes should be better. It is, in fact, a basic function of the intellectual to define the standards of good taste more clearly and to persuade people to approach them more closely. It is proper to denounce vulgarity of taste and to denounce it more strongly the more popular it is. It is permissible to reject certain desires completely as we do when by compulsory-education laws we reject the desire for illiteracy—although there is a strong presumption against the use of force in the area of tastes.

When I say that the complaints of deficiencies in tastes are misplaced when they are directed to the marketplace, I mean just that. The marketplace responds to the tastes of consumers with the goods and services that are salable, whether the tastes are elevated or depraved. It is unfair to criticize the marketplace for fulfilling these desires, when clearly the defects lie in the popular tastes themselves. I consider it a cowardly concession to a false extension of the idea of democracy to make *sub rosa* attacks on public tastes by denouncing the people who serve them. It is like blaming the waiters in restaurants for obesity.

To escape this response, the more sophisticated intellectuals have argued that people are told what to want by the marketplace—that advertising skillfully depraves and distorts popular desires. There is no doubt an element of truth in this response, but it is an element of trifling size. The advertising industry has no sovereign power to bend men's wills—we are not children who blindly follow the last announcer's instructions to rush to the store for soap. Moreover, advertising itself is a completely neutral instrument and lends itself to the dissemination of highly contradictory desires. While the automobile industry tells us not to drink while driving, the bourbon industry tells us not to drive while drinking. The symphony orchestra advertises, and gets much free publicity, in its rivalry with the dance band. Our colleges use every form of advertising, and indeed the typical university catalog would never stop Diogenes in his search for an honest man.

So I believe the intellectuals would gain in candor and in grace if they preached directly to the public instead of using advertising as a whipping boy. I believe they would gain also in virtue if they would examine their own tastes more critically; when a good comedian and a production of Hamlet are on rival channels, I wish I could be confident that less than half the professors were laughing.

The main indictment by the intellectual, however, is that the marketplace operates on the principle of self-interest, and, in fact, through competition compels even the philanthropic businessman to become self-serving. Self-interest, often described with such neutral words as egotism, greed and dog-eat-dog, is viewed as a crass, antisocial element of man's character, and an economic system that rests upon, and inculcates, this motive achieves little admiration. In fact, a dislike for profit-seeking is one of the few specific attitudes shared by the major religions.

I also find naked selfishness an unendearing trait, but I have trouble in separating it from the more admirable motives related to it. A prudent regard for one's own survival is generally applauded, even if the individual does not say, "I got out of the way of the oncoming train only to spare my Sunday School class pain." The violent endeavors of an athlete to defeat his rivals are much admired, providing the contest is more or less fair, even though the winner is expected not to say, "I am glad I won chiefly because I'm vain, but secondarily for the honor of Sheboygan High School."

Even in fields somewhat removed from the athletic arena, the roles of self-interest and what for lack of a better name I shall call benevolence are perplexingly interwoven. I have spent my life among college teachers, although admittedly in the most competitive branch of research and publication. In one sense the disinterest of my colleagues is beyond doubt: I have seen silly people—public officials as well as private, by the way—try to buy opinions, but I have not seen or even suspected any cases in which any important economist sold his professional convictions. It is also true that many of the best professors, and many of the worst, could earn more in other callings.

But on the other hand, the motives that drive them and me are not completely clear, either. When we strive to solve a scientific problem, is ambition for our own professional status completely overshadowed by our love of knowledge? I wonder. When we write an article to demonstrate the fallacies of someone else's work, is our hatred for error never mixed with a tiny bit of glee at the display of our own cleverness? I wonder.

To shift elsewhere, I have never encountered a political candidate who said: "I am running for office because I, with my dear wife and future administrative assistant, can earn more in politics than elsewhere." Nor do I expect to. But the language of public interest surely covers a good many acres of self-interest.

A major source of the view that the marketplace places special values on self-interest, beyond those more or less evident in all human behavior, is the belief that one man's gain is another's loss—that business, like the so-called friendly poker session, is a zero-sum game. Not so.

On the one hand, it must be recognized that the great source of market gains is the productivity of the participants. Unlike the poker game, the wealth of our society has been doubling even on a per capita basis every twenty-five years, and the doubling has been due to the labors and ingenuity of the men in the marketplace. Of course, there are also incomes achieved by monopoly rather than by efficiency, by fraud rather than by output, but it would be a wholly extravagant estimate that they amount to 10 per cent of the income of the marketplace. There is room for improvement here, but there is vastly more room to admire the prodigious production achievements of the marketplace.

On the other hand, I would emphasize that most of the gains from innovation in the marketplace are passed on to the community at large. A new idea may yield handsome profits for a time, but the rapid rush of competition soon drives the price of the product down to a modest level. Ball-point pens were first marketed at $12.50 to those penmen eager to write under water (and, judging by my experience, only under water); they rapidly fell in price and, as you know, are now so cheap that you have no economic excuse if you do not write the Great American Novel. Sears, Roebuck and Company and Montgomery Ward made a good deal of money in the process of improving our rural marketing structure, but I am convinced that they did more for the poor farmers of America than the sum total of the federal agricultural support programs of the last twenty-eight years.

It is an interesting illustration of the great influence of the intellectual that the marketplace itself has become apologetic of its pursuit of profit. The captains of industry now, in a world in which public relations are becoming as important as efficiency, list among their major achievements the great number of bowling alleys or college fellowships they have given to their employees. To boast that large profits demonstrate great efficiency in producing existing products and introducing new ones is considered even by them to be too archaic a form of thought for public consumption. The patron saint of economics, Adam Smith, once wrote:

> I have never known much good done by those who affected to trade for the public good. It is an affection, indeed, not very common among merchants, and very few words need to be employed in dissuading them from it.

I wonder what those very few words were.

To return to the intellectuals, their dislike for the profit motive of the marketplace no doubt rests in part on a failure to understand its logic and workings. It is a fact painful to record that the level of economic literacy has not risen noticeably in the twentieth century. Indeed, as professional economics becomes more complicated and its practitioners use an increasingly more formidable apparatus, there seems to have been retrogression in our ability to communicate with other intellectuals. Less than a century ago a treatise on economics began with a sentence such as, "Economics is a study of mankind in the ordinary business of life." Today it will often begin: "This unavoidably lengthy treatise is devoted to an examination of an economy in which the second derivatives of the utility function possess a finite number of discontinuities. To keep the problem manageable, I assume that each individual consumes only two goods, and dies after one Robertsonian week. Only elementary mathematical tools such as topology will be employed, incessantly."

But misunderstanding is not the whole explanation; I cannot believe that any amount of economic training would wholly eliminate the instinctive dislike for a system of organizing economic life through the search for profits. It will still appear to many intellectuals that a system in which men were driven by a reasonably selfless devotion to the welfare of other men would be superior to one in which they sought their own preferment. This ethic is deeply imbedded in the major religions.

I personally also believe that the good society will be populated by people who place a great value on other people's welfare. This is, however, not the only attribute of the good society, and in particular in the good society a man should be free within the widest possible limits of other men's limitations on his beliefs and actions. This great ethic of individual freedom clashes with that of benevolence, for I can seldom do positive good to another person without limiting him. I can, it is true, simply give him money, but even in this extreme case, where I seem to place no bonds on him, he inevitably faces the question of what conduct on his part will lead me to give money to him again. Usually I will find it hard to be content to do so little good—giving money to improve a man's food or housing or health will seem as inefficient as giving him gasoline so he will drive more often to museums. Hence when I give money I shall also insist that it be spent on housing, or on medical care for his children, or on growing wheat in the way that I think is socially desirable, or on the collected works of Burke and de Tocqueville or of Marx and Lenin. A patron tends to be paternalistic, in a nice way, of course. I am not saying that benevolence is bad, but that like everything else it can be carried to excess.

One final question on motives—why are they so important? Am I to admire a man who injures me in an awkward and mistaken attempt to protect me, and am I to despise a man who to earn a good income performs for me some great and lasting service? Oddly enough, I suspect our answer is that motive makes a difference —that it is less objectionable to be injured by an incompetent benefactor than by a competent villain. But I leave with you the question: Are motives as important as effects?

Several charges related to the dominance of self-interest have rounded out the intellectual's indictment of the marketplace:

First, the system makes no provision for men whose talents and interests are not oriented to profit-seeking economic activity.

Second, there are cumulative tendencies toward increasing inequality of wealth, which—if unchecked—will polarize the society into a great number of poor and a few very rich.

Third, the game in the marketplace is unfair in that inheritance of property plays an immensely larger role in success than the efforts of the individuals themselves.

I shall comment briefly on each of these assertions.

The first charge is true—the marketplace will not supply income to a man who will not supply something which people want. People have enormously varied desires, but not enough of them wish to hire men to engage in research on ancient languages nor, sixty years ago, did they hire men to study quantum mechanics. The marketplace does not provide an air force or alms for the poor. It does not even supply babies. I conclude that a society needs more than a marketplace.

The second charge, that there are cumulative tendencies to ever-increasing inequality of wealth, is untrue. I would indeed ignore the charge for fear of reprimand from the Society for the Prevention of Cruelty to Straw Men, were it not that this straw man is so popular. In plain historical fact, the inequality in the distribution of income has been diminishing, and the diminution has been due to market forces even more than to governmental efforts. It is also worth noting that a modern market economy has a less unequal income distribution than in either centrally directed or unindustrialized economies.

The third charge, that inheritance of property plays a dominant role in the distribution of income in the marketplace, is an overstatement. Inheritance of property is important, but it will give some perspective to the charge to notice that property income is only one-fifth of national income, and inherited property is less than half of all property, so less than 10 percent of all income is governed by inheritance of property.

No useful purpose would be served by trying to appraise the proper role of inheritance of property in a few passing remarks. We should have to look carefully at the effects of inheritance on incentives; we should have to look at gifts during life, which are almost equivalent to bequests; and we should have to decide whether privately endowed colleges do enough good to offset the inevitable high-living heirs—whether we can have Carleton College without having Tommy Manville.

But our greatest problem would be that inheritance extends far beyond a safe-deposit box full of bonds and stocks. I have told you that you are intelligent; I now add that the chief reason you are intelligent is that your parents are intelligent. Some of you, especially the younger of you, may find this unbelievable; Mark Twain said he was astonished by how much his father had learned during the short time it took Mark to grow from eighteen to twenty-one. But inheritance of ability is important, probably more important in its effects on the distribution of income than is the inheritance of property. So a full account of the proper role of inheritance would have to extend to ability, and perhaps even to name and reputation, as the Attorney General of the United States might agree. The social and legal institutions governing inheritance in our society are surely open to improvement, but we are unlikely to improve them if we are guided by nothing more than naïve egalitarianism.

And now to my final point. We are great believers in the human mind, we intellectuals, and its ability to conquer an ever-larger part of the immense domain of ignorance. But we have not made much use of the mind in reaching our views on the economic organization appropriate to the good society so far as its basic cultural values go. It is clear that the kinds of traits that are fostered in man are influenced by (but, of course, not only by) the way economic life is organized—after all, throughout history men have spent half their waking hours in economic activity.

Important as the moral influences of the marketplace are,

they have not been subjected to any real study. The immense proliferation of general education, of scientific progress and of democracy are all coincidental in time and place with the emergence of the free-enterprise system of organizing the market-place. I believe this coincidence was not accidental. The economic progress of the past three centuries was both cause and effect of this general growth of freedom. The dominant era of the free marketplace was in the nineteenth century. I believe, but with less confidence, that the absence of major wars in that century—the only peaceable century in history—was related to this reign of liberty. I believe, again with less confidence, that the contemporary transformation of the British public from a violent and unruly people into a population of almost painful Victorian rectitude was related to this reign of liberty.

These beliefs may be right or wrong, but they are not matters of taste. They are hypotheses concerning the relationship between economic and social organization, and are subject to analytical development and empirical testing. It is time that we did so, high time. Our ruling attitude toward the marketplace has not changed since the time of Plato. Is it not possible that it is time to rethink the question?

Part II

—

THE CASE FOR FREE ENTERPRISE

ECONOMIC CONDITIONS
FOR A FREE SOCIETY

—

By Karl Brandt*

IN any sort of permanent human association the life of a people involves economic action. Indeed, a part of their basic activities such as providing food, clothing and shelter or national defense is economic action. Even those activities which yield the most refined kind of services, such as educational, artistic, scientific or spiritual ones, are inseparable from the necessity of providing the material means for making such an output possible. This dependence of a society on the performance of its economy increases as it becomes more civilized and advances toward higher levels of consumption.

Hence it is obvious that the economic conditions under which the people must perform the major part of their activities cannot but have a decisive impact on the question whether their society can aspire to be and remain one in which freedom prevails. Next to the political order and the form of government, it is its economic system and its economic policy that determine whether a society is open and free or closed and coercive.

I do not consider it helpful or permissible to speak of a "democratic economy" and "economic democracy," as Clark Kerr has done in his part of the *Report of the United States*

* Karl Brandt, an agricultural economist, graduated from Württemburg State College of Agriculture in 1921 and received his doctorate in agriculture from the University of Berlin in 1926; the University of Heidelberg conferred an honorary degree in philosophy on him in 1951. Brandt came to the United States in 1933; from 1958 to 1961 he was a member of the President's Council of Economic Advisers, and in 1961 director of the Research Institute. He also holds membership in the American Economic Association. In 1962 Brandt served on the survey mission to the Federation of Malaya.

His writings include *Reconstruction of World Agriculture* (1945) and *The Management of Agriculture and Food in the German-Occupied and Other Areas of Fortress Europe* (1953). He has also written many articles for professional journals.

This selection is from an essay entitled *Economic Conditions for a Free Society,* and is reprinted by permission of the author.

President's Commission on the National Goals of 1960. In fact, there is a good deal of weighty evidence that institutions and procedures which are so essential to the functioning of political democracy, e.g., parliamentary procedures, ballots and referenda, are likely to have deplorable consequences if they are transferred to the sphere of decision-making in economic enterprises.

However, in this turbulent era of continual expansion of the orbit of systems of political tyranny and, even more, of coercive economic systems, it is necessary to recognize first of all the ethical motivation of the free society in the political and in the economic spheres. The concept of a noncoercive economy stands or falls—just as does the concept of a free society—with the religious faith or, if you prefer, the acceptance as an indisputable value that, unlike all other creatures in Nature, man is endowed with the divine spark of his Creator and the free will to choose between good and evil, and thereby bears responsibility for his acts. This belief alone is what gives him the potential stature of human dignity and what attributes to his life and pursuit of happiness the potential dignity of human existence. These qualities lie in the individual and his personality, with its range from failure to achievement and from the beastly to the divine. The recognition of the dignity of man makes it imperative for every citizen to do his part in preventing or remedying circumstances which subject individuals to humiliation, degradation and decay.

The efforts to define freedom and liberty merely as absence of restraint and interference by others are negative and feeble, and lead to the ideological defeat of the free society at the hands of every shade of totalitarianism. Deeply imbedded in the faith in man's free will, and the responsibility and moral obligation of choosing and making decisions which it implies, lies the inescapable consequence that in its full meaning freedom presupposes the voluntary assumption of obligations, such as self-discipline, rational control of emotions and, in general, social responsibility of the citizen, if rights are not to become an invitation to anarchy and subsequent tyranny.

The economic objective of the free society is to enable its citizens to conduct their lives in forms compatible with human dignity and to combine opportunity for economic improvement with some degree of security.

The free society and particularly the economic conditions compatible with its underlying credo imply an optimistic philosophy about individuals and society. Most of the economic action in it must depend on voluntary or free associations.

The political conditions of a free society gravitate toward the maximum decentralization of decisions and power and the anchorage of democracy in the individual; the goal of the economy of a free society calls similarly for the widest possible decentralization of decision-making and risk-bearing in freely formed combinations of human, natural and man-made resources.

The free and open society is, by definition, dynamic and deeply averse to any static stratification or guarantees for any status quo. It offers each individual the opportunity to ascend socially and economically in accordance with his development of talents, skills and moral stature, and in accordance with his contribution to the advancement of the society to which he belongs.

This requires that the economy, too, must be dynamic, bent on diminution of poverty, lifting of standards of living, improvement in the opportunity for individuals to develop their productive capacity, increase in security for individuals and families and progress in the creation of greater wealth for all. It is the antithesis of a free society to draft its members and subjugate them to a national goal of maximum output of goods and services, irrespective of whether this is done for purposes of maximizing the power of the state or for the asserted benefit of the citizenry in some more or less distant future.

Under its own ethical standards a free society cannot degrade its people to the position of production factors in calculations of national planning; it must respect them as free, active participants in the social process of the economy. Attempts to subjugate the economic policy of the free society to such goals as a specific rate of equal annual growth of the social product or of "full" employment are alien to the basic philosophy of freedom and human dignity, and defeat its purpose. Growth and reasonably high rates of employment of those willing and able to work will result from proper conditions established and fostered by the society. But any effort at forcing growth and "full" employment by government action is identical with the eventual abolition of freedom. The genuine source from which productivity increases flow is the creative mind of free people, the free play of their experimental genius and their expectation of earning the reward for risking in trial and error or in research. Centralized decisions for growth for growth's sake only are bound to lead to enormous misinvestments and misallocations of resources.

The economy of a free society can serve the idealistic and to satisfying the demands of the consumers, who exercise their freedom of choice by controlling the disposal of their income according to their own preferences and priorities. By the control over their family or household budgets, they allocate resources or factors of production to their specific uses, and determine directly and indirectly the scale of priorities in the satisfaction of their needs and wants. This holds, not only for the supply of durable and nondurable consumer goods and services, but also for producers' goods and services and the inventories of goods.

The economy of a free society can serve the idealistic and moral ends to which it is dedicated only if, first, there prevail in the institutional setting conditions for the balanced growth of the capacity to produce goods and services in line with the changing needs and the changing technology of the society; if, second, there is an optimum decentralization of decisions; and if, last, the constitution and the legislature provide for the widest possible separation of the operation of the economy from political power of the legislative and the executive branches of government.

Except in matters of military security and during periods of national emergency, the citizens of a free society must not be forced to work or to be idle, to change their jobs or their professions, to migrate or to stay where they are. In fact, not only should they not be ordered by a government to perform specific economic functions, but the prerogative as well as the duty of the citizen is to choose the type of work and the particular spot where he wants to work and live, and to accept or reject the package of conditions offered by specific employers.

The body politic of the free society must adopt an economic

policy that governs economic affairs both domestic and foreign. Such a policy requires two kinds of legislative action: (1) creation of the institutional framework of law and order for the economy and its protection by supervision and law enforcement; (2) corrective or current functional governmental assistance to the economy.

Both of these types are closely interrelated.

The free society depends, first of all, on the proper institutional setting of its economy, and on the stability and vigilant defense of such a system of law and order; and it must, second, make necessary amendments to this system wisely, cautiously and gradually.

The broad institutional setting of the economy must be an impartial legal framework which applies to all citizens and protects them against arbitrary interference by either private persons or the government. The more wisely it is arranged, the less need arises for government intervention or for sudden changes, which make for insecurity because of the perpetual risk of arbitrary decisions by government officials.

If the economy of the free society is to perform properly, its members must generally accept the institutional framework and the government's role as its protector and supporting trustee as just, equitable and fair. Once this confidence and acceptance is seriously weakened or lost, a major political emergency looms up, together with a crisis in the economy. In such situations people in their indignation over injustices may easily be tempted to accept economic solutions which involve the suspension of major freedoms.

Conversely, it is also true that the less the institutional framework of the economy is accepted by the majority of the people and the more it is subjected to sharp criticism, the more the government is bound to make use of interventions which can only operate with arbitrary executive power and coercive devices. Any revolt against even the most equitable and beneficial economic order conjures up the prospect of remedial action by dictatorial rule, irrespective of whether the revolt is based on ignorance, collusion of special interest or pressure groups, subversion from the outside or genuine grievances.

It will be shown later that the integrity of the currency of a country is of crucial importance for maintaining a high morale in a free society and faith in justice and fair play.

Before any of the major economic institutions of a free society can be discussed, it must be understood at the outset that a necessary precondition for the society's functioning at all is the existence of order and security under the law with justice for everyone. This means, very plainly, that the society must be able to enforce security of life, public health, liberty and property. As for the people themselves, they must have a sense of reasonableness in the proportions of what they expect of the economy and its possible achievements. Of even greater importance is the social conscience that pervades the free society— the urgent desire to improve the lot of the poorest among their numbers and among human beings in general.

The following institutions appear to me as the most essential ones for a free society:

The Institution of Private Property in Means of Production

Private property in every form of real estate, as well as in mobile means of production and capital, deserves the highest priority. This holds particularly for property in land for agricultural, mining, industrial, commercial or residential use in the full meaning of the sub-bundles of rights, the *jus fruendi, jus utendi* and the *jus abutendi*. The last sub-bundle includes particularly the right to encumber, to transfer title, to grant easements, to divide, to lease, to change the type of use and to bequeath to heirs.

Private property in means of production, particularly in real estate for any kind of utilization, promotes free enterprise as an essential element in the economy of a free society. The property title grants the full freedom of management and control of such a set of resources to the owner. With it he is free to organize the structure of the firm and to operate it under his exclusive decisions as a competitor in the market.

This privilege of private property in means of production and of the independence of the manager of a free enterprise is, however, inseparable from the obligation of discharging responsibilities toward the state—such as payment of taxes—and toward creditors and other claimants—such as workers and suppliers.

The free market and the free-enterprise system could not possibly provide the proper economic conditions for a society without the severity of contract law and, specifically, the laws on bankruptcy. In the free-enterprise system, profits as well as losses go to the account of the entrepreneur, with all the consequences. This system of reward and penalty leads to a movement of productive resources into the hands of business leaders who develop them to their greatest productivity and utilize them with the greatest net return. The marginal producers, i.e., those who operate with the highest costs or with the lowest efficiency, are eliminated by the vigorous test of free competition in the market.

Strangely enough, the free-enterprise system is continually under attack both for being too harsh, brutal and effective in the elimination of the unfit from the control of resources and for being a "profit system" that shelters wealthy "drones" of society. However, it is plain that in any economic system which works at all, provision is needed to insure the mobility of human resources and their shifting into activities where they can make the optimal contribution to the social product. And it is equally plain that it is to the interest of all that those who are least fit to manage economic resources efficiently should be induced to pass them along to others who are more competent and to transfer themselves to activities for which they are better qualified.

If the objective test of competition in the market is abolished and the state guarantees satisfactory prices to producers, as is the purpose of nearly all agricultural price supports, the state must not only solve the problem of adjusting the output to the demand, but also must take on the much more serious task of determining who shall be transferred to other activities. In England this has led, during and after World War II, to legal provisions for the dispossession of farmers who, county agricultural committees attested, operated below acceptable standards of efficiency. In Germany the first basic change in the institution of property in land under National Socialism, the Inheritance Farm Law of 1933, promptly established procedures by which the state could disqualify farmers as operators of family farms for a variety of reasons, including political unreliability.

A system of private property in land and free enterprise makes it necessary and desirable that some land be held in public hands.

Some beaches, parks, water reservoirs, ports, highways and roads, educational real estate, defense areas and wild-life reserves belong in this category. But it is neither necessary nor desirable that forests be publicly owned or operated, or that mineral rights or railroads' rights-of-way be retained in the public domain.

Wherever public necessities arise which make it unavoidable that private property be acquired for the government, the doctrine of eminent domain provides for such inroads on private rights by condemnation procedures. However, while this process requires public hearings as well as prompt, fair and adequate compensation to the former owners, it is a serious weakening of the free society's basic institution of private property to use eminent domain and condemnation for purposes of planning the renewal of deteriorated metropolitan areas. To deprive certain citizens of their property rights with the intent of selling them later to other citizens is an ominous departure from time-honored concepts of property. That the Supreme Court has recently declared such an extension of eminent domain as constitutional cannot but further weaken the security of the whole bundle of property rights in land.

The Market with Free Competition

Next to the institution of private property, the greatest need of a free society is a free competitive market for real estate and for producer and consumer goods and services with freely moving prices. Free-market exchange prices in consumer goods and services have multiple functions. They clear the market and inform actual and potential producers, as well as the trade and manufacturers, of the preferences of the consumer; but they also inform consumers of the relative abundance or scarcity and price worthiness of products. Freely moving market prices and the choices of consumers adjust present and future supply to effective demand.

Only in a free market, where informed and willing buyers bid in open competition for goods and services offered by informed and willing sellers, can a fair exchange value be ascertained. The greatest weakness of economic policies which deviate from or abolish the market as the price-determining institution is that they are devoid of any rational arrangement or procedure by which a price for goods or services can objectively be found. Antagonists of the market propose nothing but more or less arbitrary political and bureaucratic decisions on the price of goods or of labor. This is equally true for the concept of the *justum pretium* of the scholastics of the Middle Ages as for the Marxians, Neo-Marxians, the Christian Socialists, the apostles of the corporate state, Fascists, state capitalists and protagonists of the centrally planned economy and dirigism. None of them have any answer to the question of what criteria, other than prices being paid under the impact of demand and supply in a given market, could or should be used to determine the absolute value in terms of dollars and cents of the services of garbage removal or its relation to the value of such other services as those provided by the watchmaker, musician, mail carrier or teacher. How decisive the question of establishing the value of services is for the maintenance of a free society can best be pointed out by the consequences of fixing a certain wage for the garbage men. Since this concerns a crucial sanitation and public health service, it is obvious that if such fixed wage is too low and nobody fills the vacant job, the alternative is either to raise the offered wage until somebody accepts the job—which is the market solution— or to draft people compulsorily for such jobs—which would be the end of a free society.

Naturally, the case for the competitive economy and the market with freely moving prices begins to be seriously weakened by any compromise with its principles by the government. The worst distortions of its institutional setting that can be foisted on a competitive free-enterprise economy result from attempts to control the movements of prices and "support" them. "Price ceilings" are just as much an infraction of the market system as are "price floors," although attempts at curbing deflation are more popular than efforts at putting brakes on inflation. Both are very crude, clumsy and inadequate measures toward either goal. Yet, except for war emergencies, the vast majority of government interventions in markets are measures which impede the downward movement of prices. For the most part, marginal producers use political pressure to get a policy of governmental price support adopted, initially as a temporary, stop-disaster intervention, but soon as a permanent policy. Such pressure usually finds the spontaneous support of those who consider the market with freely moving prices under competition as a defective arrangement and who are anxious to see it abolished. Since it is the very purpose of price supports to lift prices above the level which the supply-demand forces would establish—namely, the equilibrium level—it is the logical and inevitable consequence that soon after the price supports become effective, the supply exceeds the demand. This, in turn, leads to public stockpiling and, sooner or later, to restrictive quotas, first on production and then on marketing. At this point the free economy has ended and dirigism has taken its place, although this may not be conspicuous outside the part of the economy in question. The consumer can no longer allocate resources, the producer has lost a major part of his freedom of enterprise and depends on public subsidies. Competition can no longer function properly; and, with production quotas, the otherwise highly flexible pattern of economic location of production and its distribution among enterprises and geographical regions is frozen.

Government intervention distorts the complex self-adjusting system of the market in any case; but the worst disorganization takes place when intervention takes the form of price supports—which in most cases is identical with price fixing. Since the support creates a surplus, the price can no longer rise above the support floor but "sits" tightly pinned on that floor and hence is fixed. The result is utter confusion in the market, in which all parties now receive the wrong signals. While there is a situation of surplus, price indicates a scarce supply.

The government counteracts the artificially created tendency to overproduction by acreage allotments. This unintentionally freezes the location of production, and, thus, impedes adjustments; but it is ineffective as control of output, because farmers intensify the use of the allotted acres. Hence, the next step in regimentation leads to tight marketing quotas in terms of bushels.

Price fixing by the government and the accompanying cartelization by quota allotments shift not only from price competition to political control; but they invisibly shift the responsibility for the failure or success of enterprises from their private operators to the government. It makes no difference whether the price fixing is applied to farms or to commercial and industrial enterprises.

However, since the Great Depression of the early thirties, which had its forerunner in the sharp decline in farm prices after 1928, agriculture is, in most of the Western countries, the part of the economy where the revolt against the market economy is most violent and where compulsory cartelization and prevention of competition are most popular. It is noteworthy that once a certain degree of this sort of dirigism is reached in agriculture it has a powerful tendency to spread and to infect the entire economy by expanding into more and more industries and into commerce.

This severe criticism of agricultural policies does not imply that governments cannot or should not grant temporarily self-liquidating emergency aid to farmers, but has to do primarily with the means chosen—namely, price fixing, with all its vicious effects, which distort the institutional setting of the economy and interfere with the complex, self-adjusting market mechanism. However, when the government appraises certain circumstances as a real emergency, it should not only consider price fixing as an absolute taboo, it should, then, also carefully weigh the question whether the desirable aid cannot be made available by spontaneous private initiative or, if need be, by the government's appeal to the public for such initiative. Private action can be handled with far less red tape and be better aimed at real need. It can thereby be more effective as well as more economical than governmental aid administered by inevitably bureaucratic procedures. Such spontaneous action of groups of citizens, who are able to organize even the largest relief and assistance campaigns, fits ideally into the functions of a truly free society. With the numerous foundations, privately endowed universities, churches, civic clubs and the multitude of other private associations, there is hardly any need for calling the government into social aid or relief action, except in the extreme emergency of war or disasters, such as earthquakes. Indeed, the more the citizens of a free society tend to call for government action for social aid of every sort, the faster they reach the end of what they cherish—freedom.

The Necessity for a Market Police

It is just as unrealistic and futile to conceive of a free market without law enforcement by a competent and alert market police as it would be to assume that one could have public order or the security of private property without a police force, or that traffic on rivers or seas or land or in the air could move freely without effective policing. Even during the Middle Ages it was common practice for kings and princes to protect regular markets by supervising measures and weights and inflicting severe penalties for fraudulent practices. In this century the establishment of publicly supervised and standardized measures for quality and enforcement of open display of prices have given prices more precision and effectiveness.

But far more is needed in law enforcement to keep a free-enterprise system and a market economy functioning in a free society. The whole idea that a market economy is one which the state can leave alone and where the society can rely simply on the purifying power of competition is absurd. In fact, the claim that the market economy with freedom of competition means laissez faire and laissez aller is nothing but a Marxian indictment and a caricature designed to ridicule. It should be recognized as such by all combatants for the free society. In the battle for freedom it is just as fatal to define it negatively as the absence of restraint by others as it is to envisage a viable free economy under a feeble watchman-state with a laissez-faire philosophy in economics. A free economy needs not only responsible and self-disciplined individuals and groups but also a powerful state which endorses the philosophy of an open market with freely moving prices, free competition and free enterprise, a state which is determined to keep the economy healthy, strong, expanding and free. Of course, the state must refrain from engaging in business itself, not only in order to avoid competing unfairly with the private economy, but to keep its bureaucracy small, dedicated to civil service in support of the free economy and free from corruption. The state must do its part to generate the general conditions in which the market economy can flourish, and it must be determined to police it against adulteration of the principles on which it stands.

A free competitive market does not remain free or competitive by its own momentum. The temptation to reap special benefits by restraining competition or excluding it is too great. Hence, it is the inescapable duty of the free society to use the law enforcement and regulatory power of the government to protect the consumers as well as the entire economy against those who arrogate to themselves the right to change the institutional setting of a competitive free market to their benefit and to the detriment of the consumers and of the competing producers. This means continual vigilance and breaking up of monopolistic arrangements from whatever side they may come: from industrial or commercial trusts or cartels; from consumers' or farmers' cooperative associations; from labor unions; and from any other organization.

Further Basic Economic Functions of the State

For the productivity, performance and growth of its economy, the free society must rely first and last on the private initiative, resourcefulness, inventive genius and common sense of its people, and on the supervisory and assistance functions of the state, particularly in cases of national or regional calamities. However, the state has to perform other basic economic functions of a sovereign without which the private-enterprise system and the market cannot flourish.

The first function is to provide a sound monetary and banking policy which maintains a strong, stable, freely convertible currency: an adequate volume of money and an adequate flow of savings and credit. The second function consists of a constructive conduct of the government's own household or a fiscal policy which is compatible with a strong free economy.

Both functions are closely interrelated, and both are of vital importance for maintaining a free economy and for stability and healthy growth. Both are the most essential instruments of public policy toward diminishing the violence of inflationary or deflationary swings of economic activity.

The most typical worldwide economic phenomenon of the period since the beginning of World War I is that in all democratically governed countries, and even more so in most of the dictatorships, the political pressures for state intervention, subsidies and social aid have led to the depreciation of national currencies. From the twenties to the latter part of the fifties, manipulation of currencies, foreign-exchange controls and quantitative restrictions of imports have abrogated more and more of the functions of a market economy and with it the curtailment of political freedom. Since 1958 a new era of convertibility of major currencies has begun, and competition has become more active among industrial countries.

For the present discussion it seems crucial to recognize that hardly any other development has played as devastating a role in the destruction of government by law and of freedom as has the inflation of currencies in the Western countries. There is an abundance of incontrovertible evidence that the most powerful influence that laid the psychological foundations for the era of nihilism in Germany under Hitler was the progressive and, in the end, total depreciation of the currency after World War I. It is most likely that many of the negative attitudes of French citizens toward their country or their government have their roots in the inflationary policies of the French Revolution and the repeated experience of the population with inflation up to these days.

Even in the United States, with a much slower pace of inflation, the point was reached in 1958 or 1959 where sudden massive shifts in the general public's preference toward certain supposedly inflation-proof forms of savings indicated a dangerous loss of confidence in the stability of the currency. Since the unit of the national currency is the measure of all values, and price inflation distorts or destroys all relations between values of long-term obligations and current values of goods and services, the entire heirarchy of values becomes disorganized. The worst feature is that a relatively small number of people find ways and means to protect themselves from losses due to inflation and even gain by it substantially at the expense of the majority. Among the losers are all those who depend for their livelihood on life insurance, savings, pensions, income from fixed-interest securities or from mortgages. This corrodes the faith of the people in a free society, in the essential fairness and justice of the free-enterprise and market system, a faith which is the real foundation on which the economy of a free society must be anchored. Inflation diverts the flow of investment from places of greatest need toward places of greatest security, and it thereby retards economic development.

Hence, the greatest support a government can give a free economy is to conduct its own household in a fashion that keeps the currency strong and its purchasing power stable; to refrain, by its own deficit financing and borrowing, from depreciating the supply of investment capital for the private economy; and to use its power of adjusting the reserve requirements for banks and changing the discount rates to prevent excessive expansion or contraction of the flow of credit and of the money supply.

Since the free society must be interested in the preservation and improvement of peaceful relations with other nations, it is essential that it maintain an optimal exchange of goods, services and capital with other countries. To give such relations the greatest stability requires reliance on long-term treaties and agreements and a minimum of administrative discretion in effecting short-term changes. From that angle, fixed rates of customs duties are far superior to flexible rates or quotas. Unfortunately, too many of the protagonists of private enterprise, while giving lip service to the general principle of comparative advantage and competition in foreign trade, argue for protection as soon as their own products are in some way affected.

Containment of Expansion of the Public Sector

Inherent in the economic development of nearly all countries with decentralized political power is the tendency for government expenditure to absorb an increasing proportion of the total gross national product or expenditures. This raises a serious problem for a free society, because the larger this public share becomes, the more the forces of free competition will be weakened and political command and control over parts of the market economy will expand. Political freedom is also seriously jeopardized by an increase in the part of the electorate which consists of government employees with a vested interest in more public expenditures.

The possibility of containing this disproportionate growth of public expenditures hangs chiefly on the determination of the people of the free society to confine the services and functions of the government strictly to those activities which cannot be performed equally well or better by private enterprise. Beyond such self-restraint of the citizens vis-à-vis the temptation of trying to get something for nothing from their government, the main hope for containment of the expansion of the public sector rests upon the eventually stiffening resistance against excessive taxation. Unfortunately, the growth of the share of government expenditures in the gross national product since 1941 has been pushed up chiefly by the exorbitant costs of national defense. This is, however, the kind of public service to which the members of a free society are hesitant to apply primarily economic concepts. The temptation is great for the legislative and executive branches of government to solve such eminently social and economic problems as increasing employment and accelerating the output of goods and services via the military detour of appropriating large funds for the production of better weapons and more ordnance stocks. Since the actual situation of the state defense and the evaluation of the true necessity to expand the defense budget remain secret, it is doubtful how much the public can actually do to prevent the further growth of this part of the government's budget. Sheer resistance against a rise in taxation which the people consider excessive or unbearable might be the best constraining influence. But this would not prohibit the expansion of public expenditures by deficit financing and continuing rise in the public debt for many years. Such an inflationary policy, as has been mentioned earlier, would eventually undermine the economy of the free society.

The jeopardy to a free society which derives from the breathtaking pace of technological change in the means of total war is increasing, not only because some extremely expensive weapons become obsolete before they can actually be delivered to the armed forces, but because of the literally astronomical scope of activities in the so-called cold war of nerves or prestige. The race to the moon with rockets illustrates the point. Moreover, with the vast scope of defense orders, including research and development of weapons, the legitimate business interests of the captains of industry and commerce begin to be so much influenced on behalf of larger congressional appropriations for defense purposes and expansion of governmental purchase of goods and services that they are no longer free to judge the public interest where the defense budget is involved. This makes it particularly important that control over defense measures remain in the legislative branch of government and that all economic aspects be thoroughly aired in public.

The Problems of Redistribution of Income and Wealth

While free competition and free enterprise make an economy far more productive than any coercive system, it is also true that the abundance of production and the growth of the statistical average of the social product per capita does not prevent the possible development of exorbitant differentials in income as well as wealth. These tend to weaken the morale and the concepts of social justice of a free society. Such weakening of the moral fiber of a free society begins particularly once some second- or third-generation heirs of former leaders in economic activities, who inherited huge fortunes and incomes, make irresponsible and offensive use of it, or no use at all, and fail to live up to the obligations of wealth.

The far greater jeopardy to the economic conditions compatible with a lasting, strong and dynamic free society derives, however, from the fact that the accumulation of giant blocks of wealth inevitably bestows on its owners extraordinary economic and concomitant political power. It can be used in ways which undermine the foundations of the free society, the more so when those who control such wealth no longer feel morally bound by the humanistic philosophy and ethics which are its foundations.

Ways of keeping the emergence of such exorbitant social inequities within bounds compatible with the requirements of maintaining a free-enterprise economy must be sought within the government's fiscal policies. In order to arrive at equitable property taxes, the market gives far more objective criteria than any assessments which emancipate values from market prices. If property taxes are fitted into the market-price structure, they provide a key to an equitable distribution of the burden, provided there are no class or caste privileges in assessment or collection. Death duties or inheritance taxes play an important role in preventing the perpetuation of vast private accumulations of wealth. However, in imposing property taxes, as well as death duties, extreme caution should be exercised in order to avoid weakening the incentive to production and investment or the very loyalty of the citizenry by too sharp a bite and too steep progressions.

Conclusion

The economic conditions for a free society can be properly determined only by recognizing the moral foundations of such a society as well as the nature and order of importance of the resources at its disposal. Freedom is inseparable from human dignity; this rules out the pursuit of purely materialistic goals and, even more, the coercive use of man as a tool toward such ends. A free society, likewise, cannot dispense with a social conscience in establishing its economic institutions and shaping its policies. In evaluating its productive economic capacity, the free society stands or falls with the belief that free individuals are more productive workers than slaves. But the free-enterprise economy can be fully productive and perform better than the coercive economy of state capitalism, dirigism or the corporative state only if the people accept the competitive market order, and only if they understand the necessity for a considerable degree of mobility of resources, including manpower, as well as the benefits derived from such adjustment. They must accept the responsibility of their own initiative, they must be reasonable in their expectations as to the rate of possible progress and, as income earners, they must use their freedom to allocate their money with thrift for consumption, savings and investment. They must have a sense of worth of the freedom and the extraordinary opportunities the market economy grants as compensation for the risk and inevitable hardship of the competitive market. Without such an attitude, the economic conditions for a free society cannot be fulfilled.

Whether the area of the free market economy can be expanded in combat with the enormously well-organized propaganda drive of the Soviet bloc throughout the world will be decided, not by the splendid actual performance of the free economies and the failure of the coercive economies to solve even their food problem, but by the success or failure of the free countries in educating the public in general about the real issues and by the success or failure of the peoples of free societies in carrying the ideological offensive for the free economy into all countries, including those under totalitarian rule.

THE ADVANTAGES OF A FREE–
ENTERPRISE PRICE SYSTEM

—

By W. Allen Wallis*

ALMOST everyone says he is in favor of free enterprise, but hardly anyone really is. Slogans like "Make Free Enterprise Work" or "Preserve Capitalism" are the usual rallying cries of all kinds of programs to impair freedom of enterprise. A lot of this is disingenuous.

These disingenuous slogans of the false friends of free enterprise don't bother me nearly as much as the fact that many real friends of free enterprise have hazy notions about how such a system is supposed to work. Even they fail to understand that most so-called welfare objectives can be achieved better by free enterprise than by collectivism. In debate they are too often easy pushovers for the collectivists.

I am continually impressed by the fact that most individualists and most collectivists are surprisingly close together in their general objectives of social welfare—elimination of poverty, reduction of inequality and provision for hardship. The differences between the individualists and the collectivists are differences, not in values, but in technical analysis of the means of attaining these values.

For this reason, I shall attempt to picture in very broad strokes

---

* Wilson Allen Wallis, president of the University of Rochester, received his A.B. from the University of Minnesota in 1932, and was a fellowship student at the University of Chicago from 1933 to 1935 and at Columbia University 1935–36. In 1946 he became professor of statistics and economics at the University of Chicago, then chairman of the department of statistics and dean of the Graduate School of Business. Wallis served as executive vice-chairman of the Cabinet Committee for Price Stability and Economic Growth from 1959 to 1961.

He was co-compiler, with Frank H. Knight, of *The Ethics of Competition and Other Essays* (1935); editor of the *Journal* of the American Statistical Association 1950–59; and chairman of the editorial board of the *New Encyclopedia of Social Sciences* in 1961.

The following article was originally presented as a speech; it appeared with minor changes in the July, 1957, *Freeman*.

the basic mechanism of a free enterprise economy—to describe the way it should work and mostly does. . . .

Here in the U.S. is an area of about 3,000,000 square miles containing 150,000,000 people. Suppose you were asked how to organize these people to utilize the resources available to them for their material satisfactions. You can imagine you have a fairly detailed inventory of the natural resources of the country, of the people and their knowledge, energies and abilities and of their wants. Imagine that all these resources are as unorganized as a set of chessmen just poured out of their box and awaiting organization on the chessboard. Your problem is to organize the resources so that wants will be filled as well as possible.

If you can get your head working at all in the face of so staggering a prospect, it will occur to you that one of the first things you are going to need is some way of establishing goals and measuring achievement. Which of the many things wanted are going to be produced, in what quantities, and with what priorities?

After you establish these goals and priorities, you will need a method of assigning the various pieces of capital, the various natural resources and the various people to particular activities. Each will have several alternative uses; you will need a method of deciding which use to assign it or him to, and of coordinating the resources assigned to cooperate in each task.

Then, third, you will have to have some system for dividing the product among the people: who gets how much of what, and when?

Fourth, you will probably realize that for one reason or another your system will not work absolutely perfectly, but will sometimes turn out to have overproduced some things and to have underproduced others. You will need some system of adjustment to these temporary shortages and abundances, until your method of measuring achievement and your method of allocating resources can get the basic situation corrected.

A fifth kind of problem you may worry about is that of providing for the expansion and improvement of your capital, equipment and technological knowledge.

These five functions have to be provided for when you establish any organization, even a small and relatively simple one.

When we consider the large and complex organization of an entire economy, what are some of the alternative ways of arranging for them?

The most obvious way to arrange things is the way an army does. You set up a commander or a general staff. They decide on goals, they decide who shall do what to attain them, they decide how to apportion the product; and they issue orders accordingly. Another method is that used in beehives and ant colonies, in which caste and custom determine who does what. Things go on in the same way, generation after generation.

A third way is to introduce money and let each person decide what activities that others will pay for he will engage in, and what things that others offer for money he will buy. This is a method that no one really invented. It requires careful and sometimes complicated analysis to discover how it will really work. Indeed, it was only with the recognition that this is in fact a method of organizing society that the scientific study of economics began, back in 1776.

Under this system, goals are set by the money offers of individuals for goods and services. Resources are allocated to one activity or another by the desires of their owners for money income. Goods are distributed to individuals according to their willingness and ability to pay the prices. Thus prices become the crucial organizing element in such an economy. Indeed, this system is often called the "price system."

The price system has two outstanding features. First, it is by all odds the most efficient system of social organization ever conceived. It makes it possible for huge multitudes to cooperate effectively, multitudes who may hardly know of each other's existence, or whose personal attitudes toward one another may be indifference or hostility. Second, it affords a maximum of individual freedom and a minimum of coercion. And since people can cooperate effectively in production even when their attitudes on other issues are hostile, there is no need for unity and conformity in religion, politics, recreation and language—or even in patriotism and goodwill, except in the very broadest senses.

Although one of the big features of the price system that commends it is the voluntary nature of individual actions, the system nevertheless exerts powerful inducements and even compulsions.

A consumer who has it in mind to use up a lot of a scarce commodity highly prized by others is forced to forego consuming other commodities to an extent judged by others to be equivalent. A producer who tries to get more income than his services are judged by others to be worth is prevented from doing so by the freedom of buyers to buy elsewhere and of other sellers to underprice him. A business manager who tries to waste labor, capital and raw materials, either by producing something less desired than other things that could be made with the labor, capital and raw materials or by using the labor, capital and raw materials inefficiently, is prevented from doing so because he will find himself taking in less money than he pays out. As long as he can make good the deficit by giving up his own right to consume, this can continue; but when he can no longer make good —that is, when he can no longer pay for the labor, capital and raw materials—he is forced to stop wasting them just as firmly as if a cease-and-desist order were issued by a federal bureau of efficiency. Maybe more firmly, for his congressman may be more influential with the federal bureau than with his creditors.

The freedom of the system produces inducements or compulsions for individuals to act efficiently in the general interest. It is not by any means true that each enterprise is free to do what it pleases. It is restricted by the freedom of consumers to buy elsewhere; of the owners of labor, capital and raw materials to sell elsewhere; and of business managers to enter the same business in competition with it.

This freedom of others to compete for advantages is effective in checking individual self-aggrandizement, because economic information is effectively disseminated by prices. Prices represent one of the most efficient communication devices ever invented.

Indeed, we might look on the problem of organization as hinging on communication. The problem is to bring to bear on each decision two very different kinds of information. On the one hand, any decision depends on general, overall economic data; for example, how much a certain product is wanted and how abundant the resources are from which it could be made. On the other hand, it depends on minute special knowledge; for example, knowledge of peculiar abilities, of unused resources, of possible changes in ways of doing things.

Now the problem is whether to transmit the detailed knowledge of special circumstances to a central agency, or to transmit the general information to the individuals who have the detailed knowledge. The detailed knowledge is too voluminous and nebulous for transmittal or for assimilation, and no one could know what parts should be selected. The general information, however, is summarized in prices.

Just that part of the general data that is relevant to an individual's decision is summarized in prices. If a price goes up, that tells him everything he needs to know to guide his action; he does not need to know why the price went up; the fact that it did go up tells him to try to use a little less or it tells him to produce more of the commodity, and how far to go in his efforts.

Not only do prices convey information on how an individual *should* act, but they provide at the same time a powerful inducement for him to do so.

In conclusion, let me acknowledge that I have given only a sketch, and only of an ideal free-enterprise or price system, at that. I do not apologize for that, however, for an understanding of the theory of a price system is essential to any efforts to improve our economic organization or to any comparison of alternative modes of economic organization. To me the most depressing thing about the prospects for a free society is not the hydrogen bomb, or international politics or communist agitation; it is the fact that so very few have any understanding of economics.

THE MORAL ELEMENT
IN FREE ENTERPRISE

—

By F. A. Hayek*

ECONOMIC activity provides the material means for all our ends. At the same time, most of our individual efforts are directed to providing means for the ends of others in order that they, in turn, may provide us with the means for our ends. It is only because we are free in the choice of our means that we are also free in the choice of our ends.

Economic freedom is thus an indispensable condition of all other freedom, and free enterprise both a necessary condition and a consequence of personal freedom. In discussing the moral element in free enterprise I shall, therefore, not confine myself to the problems of economic life but consider the general relations between freedom and morals.

By freedom in this connection I mean, in the great Anglo-Saxon tradition, independence of the arbitrary will of another. This is the classical conception of freedom under the law, a state of affairs in which a man may be coerced only where coercion is required by the general rules of law, equally applicable to all, and never by the discretionary decision of administrative authority.

The relationship between this freedom and moral values is mutual and complex. I shall therefore have to confine myself to

* Friedrich von Hayek, professor of economics at the University of Freiburg (Germany) since 1962, received his J.U.D. from the University of Vienna in 1921, and the D.S. (economics) from the University of London in 1943. He was Tooke professor of economic science and statistics at the University of London 1931–50, and professor of social and moral science at the University of Chicago 1950–62.

Among Hayek's books are *Capitalism and the Historians* (1954) and *The Constitution of Liberty* (1960).

This selection was originally presented to a symposium on the spiritual and moral significance of free enterprise at the 66th National Congress of American Industry, December 6, 1961. It is reprinted by permission of the National Association of Manufacturers.

bringing out the salient points in something like telegraphic style.

It is, on the one hand, an old discovery that morals and moral values will grow only in an environment of freedom, and that, in general, moral standards of people and classes are high only where they have long enjoyed freedom—and proportional to the amount of freedom they have possessed. It is also an old insight that a free society will work well only where free action is guided by strong moral beliefs and, therefore, that we shall enjoy all the benefits of freedom only where freedom is already well established. To this I want to add that freedom, if it is to work well, requires not only strong moral standards but moral standards of a particular kind, and that it is possible in a free society for moral standards to grow up which, if they become general, will destroy freedom and with it the basis of all moral values.

Before I turn to this point, which is not generally understood, I must briefly elaborate upon two old truths which ought to be familiar but which are often forgotten. That freedom is the matrix required for the growth of moral values—indeed, not merely one value among many but the source of all values—is almost self-evident. It is only where the individual has choice, and its inherent responsibility, that he has occasion to affirm existing values, to contribute to their further growth and to earn moral merit. Obedience has moral value only where it is a matter of choice and not of coercion. It is in the order in which we rank our different ends that our moral sense manifests itself; and in applying the general rules of morals to particular situations each individual is constantly called upon to interpret and apply the general principles and in doing so to create particular values.

I have no time here for showing how this has in fact brought it about that free societies not only have generally been law-abiding societies but also, in modern times, have been the source of all the great humanitarian movements aiming at active help to the weak, the ill and the oppressed. Unfree societies, on the other hand, have as regularly developed a disrespect for the law, a callous attitude to suffering and even sympathy for the malefactor.

I must turn to the other side of the medal. It should also be obvious that the results of freedom must depend on the values which free individuals pursue. It would be impossible to assert that a free society will always and necessarily develop values of which we would approve, or even, as we shall see, that it will maintain values which are compatible with the preservation of freedom. All that we can say is that the values we hold are the product of freedom, that in particular the Christian values had to assert themselves through men who successfully resisted coercion by government and that it is to the desire to be able to follow one's own moral convictions that we owe the modern safeguards of individual freedom. Perhaps we can add to this that only societies which hold moral values essentially similar to our own have survived as free societies, while in others freedom has perished.

All this provides a strong argument why it is most important that a free society be based on strong moral convictions and why, if we want to preserve freedom *and* morals, we should do all in our power to spread the appropriate moral convictions. But what I am mainly concerned with is the error that men must first be good before they can be granted freedom.

It is true that a free society lacking a moral foundation would be a very unpleasant society in which to live. But it would, even so, be better than a society which is unfree and immoral; and it at least offers the hope of a gradual emergence of moral convictions, which an unfree society prevents. On this point I am afraid I strongly disagree with John Stuart Mill, who maintained that until men have attained the capacity of being guided to their own improvement by conviction or persuasion, "there is nothing for them but implicit obedience to an Akbar or Charlemagne, if they are so fortunate as to find one." Here I believe T. B. Macaulay expressed the much greater wisdom of an older tradition, when he wrote that "many politicians of our time are in the habit of laying it down as a self-evident proposition that no people are to be free till they are fit to use their freedom. The maxim is worthy of the fool in the old story, who resolved not to go into the water till he had learned to swim. If men are to wait for liberty till they become wise and good, they may indeed wait forever."

But I must now turn from what is merely the reaffirmation of old wisdom to more critical issues. I have said that liberty, to work well, requires not merely the existence of strong moral convictions but also the acceptance of particular moral views. By this I do *not* mean that within limits utilitarian considerations will contribute to alter moral views on particular issues. Nor do I mean that, as Edwin Cannan expressed it, "of the two principles, Equity and Economy, Equity is ultimately the weaker; . . . the judgment of mankind about what is equitable is liable to change, and . . . one of the forces that causes it to change is mankind's discovery from time to time that what was supposed to be quite just and equitable in some particular matter had become, or perhaps always was, uneconomical."

This is also true and important, though it may not be a commendation to all people. I am concerned rather with some more general conceptions which seem to me essential conditions of a free society and without which it cannot survive. The two crucial ones seem to me the belief in individual responsibility and the approval as just of an arrangement by which material rewards are made to correspond to the value which a person's particular services have to his fellows, *not* to the esteem in which he is held as a whole person for his moral merit.

I must be brief on the first point—which I find very difficult. Modern developments here are part of the story of the destruction of moral value by scientific error, which has recently been my chief concern—and what a scholar happens to be working on at the moment tends to appear to him as the most important subject in the world. But I shall try to say what belongs here in a very few words.

Free societies have always been societies in which the belief in individual responsibility has been strong. They have allowed individuals to act on *their* knowledge and beliefs and have treated the results achieved as due to them. The aim was to make it worthwhile for people to act rationally and reasonably and to persuade them that what they would achieve depended chiefly on them. This last belief is undoubtedly not entirely correct, but it certainly had a wonderful effect in developing both initiative and circumspection.

By a curious confusion it has come to be thought that this belief in individual responsibility has been refuted by growing insight into the manner in which events generally, and human actions in particular, are determined by certain classes of causes.

It is probably true that we have gained increasing understanding of the *kinds* of circumstances which affect human action—but no more. We can certainly not say that a particular conscious act of any man is the necessary result of particular circumstances that we can specify—leaving out his peculiar individuality built up by the whole of history. Of our generic knowledge as to how human action can be influenced we make use in assessing praise and blame—which we do for the purpose of making people behave in a desirable fashion. It is on this limited determinism—as much as our knowledge in fact justifies—that the belief in responsibility is based, while only a belief in some metaphysical self which stands outside the chain of cause and effect could justify the contention that it is useless to hold the individual responsible for his actions.

Yet, crude as is the fallacy underlying the opposite and supposedly scientific view, it has had the most profound effect in destroying the chief device which society has developed to assure decent conduct—the pressure of opinion making people observe the rules of the game. And it has ended in that "myth of mental illness" which a distinguished psychiatrist, Dr. T. S. Szasz, has recently justly castigated in a book so titled. We have probably not yet discovered the best way of teaching people to live according to rules which make life in society for them and their fellows not too unpleasant. But in our present state of knowledge I am sure that we shall never build up a successful free society without that pressure of praise and blame which treats the individual as responsible for his conduct and also makes him bear the consequences of even innocent error.

But if it is essential for a free society that the esteem in which a person is held by his fellows depends on how far he lives up to the demand for moral law, it is also essential that material reward should *not* be determined by the opinion of his fellows of his moral merits but by the value which they attach to the particular services he renders them. This brings me to my second chief point: the conception of social justice which must prevail if a free society is to be preserved. This is the point on which the defenders of a free society and the advocates of a collectivist system are chiefly divided. And on this point, while the advocates of the socialist conception of distributive justice are usually very outspoken, the upholders of freedom are unnecessarily shy about stating bluntly the implications of their ideal.

The simple facts are these: We want the individual to have liberty because only if *he* can decide what to do can he also use all his unique combination of information, skills and capacities, which nobody else can fully appreciate. To enable the individual to fulfill his potential we must also allow him to act on his own estimates of the various chances and probabilities. Since we do not know what he knows, we cannot decide whether his decisions were justified; nor can we know whether his success or failure was due to his efforts and foresight, or to good luck. In other words, we must look at results, not intentions or motives, and can allow him to act on his own knowledge only if we also allow him to keep what his fellows are willing to pay him for his services, irrespective of whether we think this reward appropriate to the moral merit he has earned or the esteem in which we hold him as a person.

Such remuneration, in accordance with the value of a man's services, inevitably is often very different from what we think of his moral merit. This, I believe, is the chief source of the dissatisfaction with a free-enterprise system and of the clamor for "distributive justice." It is neither honest nor effective to deny that there is such a discrepancy between the moral merit and esteem which a person may earn by his actions and, on the other hand, the value of the services for which we pay him. We place ourselves in an entirely false position if we try to gloss over this fact or to disguise it. Nor have we any need to do so.

It seems to me one of the great merits of a free society that material reward is *not* dependent on whether the majority of our fellows like or esteem us personally. This means that, so long as we keep within the accepted rules, moral pressure can be brought on us only through the esteem of those whom we ourselves respect and not through the allocation of material reward by a social authority. It is of the essence of a free society that we should be materially rewarded, not for doing what others order us to do, but for giving them what they want. Our conduct ought certainly to be guided by our desire for their esteem. But we are free because the success of our daily efforts does not depend on whether particular people like us, or our principles, or our religion, or our manners, and because *we* can decide whether the material reward others are prepared to pay for our services makes it worthwhile for us to render them.

We seldom know whether a brilliant idea which a man suddenly conceives, and which may greatly benefit his fellows, is the result of years of effort and preparatory investment, or whether it is a sudden inspiration induced by an accidental combination of knowledge and circumstance. But we do know that, where in a given instance it has been the former, it would not have been worthwhile to take the risk if the discoverer were not allowed to reap the benefit. And since we do not know how to distinguish one case from the other, we must also allow a man to get the gain when his good fortune is a matter of luck.

I do not wish to deny, I rather wish to emphasize, that in our society personal esteem and material success are much too closely bound together. We ought to be much more aware that if we regard a man as entitled to a high material reward, that in itself does not necessarily entitle him to high esteem. And, though we are often confused on this point, it does not mean that this confusion is a necessary result of the free-enterprise system—or that in general the free-enterprise system is more materialistic than other social orders. Indeed, and this brings me to the last point I want to make, it seems to me in many respects considerably less so.

In fact, free enterprise has developed the only kind of society which, while it provides us with ample material means, if that is what we mainly want, still leaves the individual free to choose between material and nonmaterial reward. The confusion of which I have been speaking—between the value which a man's services have to his fellows and the esteem he deserves for his moral merit—*may* well make a free-enterprise society materialistic. But the way to prevent this is certainly not to place the control of all material means under a single direction, to make the distribution of material goods the chief concern of all common effort and thus to get politics and economics inextricably mixed.

It is at least possible for a free-enterprise society to be in this respect a pluralistic society which knows no single order of rank but has many different principles on which esteem is based;

where worldly success is neither the only evidence nor regarded as certain proof of individual merit. It may well be true that periods of a very rapid increase of wealth, in which many enjoy the benefits of wealth for the first time, tend to produce for a time a predominant concern with material improvement. Until the recent European upsurge many members of the more comfortable classes there used to decry as materialistic the economically more active periods to which they owed the material comfort which had made it easy for them to devote themselves to other things.

Periods of great cultural and artistic creativity have generally followed, rather than coincided with, the periods of the most rapid increase in wealth. To my mind this shows *not* that a free society must be dominated by material concerns but rather that with freedom it is the moral atmosphere in the widest sense, the values which people hold, which will determine the chief direction of their activities. Individuals as well as communities, when they feel that other things have become more important than material advance, can turn to them. It is certainly not by the endeavor to make material reward correspond to all merit but only by frankly recognizing that there are other and often more important goals than material success that we can guard ourselves against becoming too materialistic.

Surely it is unjust to blame a system as more materialistic because it leaves it to the individual to decide whether he prefers material gain to other kinds of excellence, instead of having this decided for him. There is indeed little merit in being idealistic if the provision of the material means required for these idealistic aims is left to somebody else. It is only where a person can himself choose to make a material sacrifice for a nonmaterial end that he deserves credit. The desire to be relieved of the choice, and of any need for personal sacrifice, certainly does not seem to me particularly idealistic.

I must say that I find the atmosphere of the advanced welfare state in every sense more materialistic than that of a free-enterprise society. If the latter gives individuals much more scope to serve their fellows by the pursuit of purely materialistic aims, it also gives them the opportunity to pursue any other aim they regard as more important. One must remember, however, that the pure idealism of an aim is questionable whenever the material means necessary for its fulfillment have been created by others.

In conclusion, I want for a moment to return to the point from which I started. When we defend the free-enterprise system we must always remember that it deals only with means. What we make of our freedom is up to us. We must not confuse efficiency in providing means with the purposes which they serve. A society which has no other standard than efficiency will indeed waste that efficiency. If men are to be free to use their talents to provide us with the means we want, we must remunerate them in accordance with the value these means have to us. Nevertheless, we ought to esteem them only in accordance with the use they make of the means at their disposal.

Let us encourage usefulness to one's fellows by all means, but let us not confuse it with the importance of the ends which men ultimately serve. It is the glory of the free-enterprise system that it makes it at least possible that each individual, while serving his fellows, can do so for his own ends. But the system is itself only a means, and its infinite possibilities must be used in the service of ends which exist apart.

Part III

—

THE ESSENTIALS OF THE SYSTEM

SECTION 1
PRIVATE PROPERTY

THE VITAL IMPORTANCE
OF PROPERTY RIGHTS
—
By Gottfried Dietze*

PROPERTY rights are very fundamental rights. This conclusion follows from an examination of the living process and of primitive associations.

Scholars have demonstrated that property is an institution of nature and prior to all human organization, and that its naturalness is evident in an examination of plant and animal life. Even the most primitive forms of life have been found to possess property. A plant has a particular piece of earth for its property, which is occupied by its roots. If deprived of its soil, the plant will die. A plant defends its property. Its roots protect the piece of ground which they occupy from invasions. Some plants protect themselves still more vigorously. Possessing thorns and bristles, or the capacity to secrete fluids which kill approaching animals, they protect the very space above the ground in which they grow. Thus on the most rudimentary level of life, property is essential to life itself, and protected accordingly.

The situation is analogous in animal life. An animal has its cover, refuge or cave as a prerequisite for its existence. It defends this property. Whether vegetarian or carnivorous, animals have their own territory, and they keep out those that attempt to encroach upon it. Food is not only collected for immediate consumption, but often is stored and defended as property. The apiarist who takes honey from the hives shields his skin to avoid being stung for a deprivation of property. Most of us have learned a lesson when trying to take away a dog's bone.

* Gottfried Dietze, professor of political science at John Hopkins University, holds doctorates in law from the University of Heidelberg, in politics from Princeton University and in juridical science from the University of Virginia. In addition to *In Defense of Property* (1963), from which the following article is taken, he is the author of *The Federalist: A Classic on Federalism* and *Free Government* (1960).

"The Vital Importance of Property Rights" is reprinted by permission of Henry Regnery Company and the author.

Finally, property is one of the first values of which men are aware. By instinct or reasoning, a child wants to have things. Primitive men have their dwelling and a territory on which they feed, be it through hunting or agricultural pursuits. They are prerequisites of their existence. A primitive man collects his livelihood in excess of what he can consume for the sake of "saving it for a rainy day" or for that of exchanging it for other goods. Aware of the value of his property and the necessity for its protection, he will put it in a safe place.

Property is also essential for freedom. The plant which is uprooted has not only its life endangered, but, also, its freedom to grow is threatened. An animal deprived of food not only starves to death, but also lacks freedom of action. If a man is deprived of his property, then the development of his personality is retarded. It does not matter whether only his immediate necessities, or what he has stored for later consumption or exchange are taken away. Although depriving him of his immediate necessities threatens his life, the removal of any property would be just as detrimental, because it would threaten his free development and thus his freedom of existence.

Property is intimately related to life and freedom. It is a prerequisite of the freedom to be and to act. It is as old as life and freedom, and also as important. Property rights are thus distinguishable from such rights as freedom of religion, of speech, of the press, of assembly and association, freedom from arbitrary arrest and so forth. For these rights were not present at the beginning of life. Furthermore, originally they did not enjoy a status equal to that of life and of freedom. It is not necessary to prove this assertion in the cases of plant and animal life. And it scarcely seems required with respect to man. While men may have been aware of the value of these rights at a primitive stage of their development, they did not consider them as immediate necessities for their existence.

The importance of property from a biological point of view is matched by its importance for society. It may be argued that the mere fact that property is a prerequisite for the survival of men, and is thus a truly natural right, does not entail that the institution of private property must also be sanctioned once men have formed societies, since under the new conditions the survival of the species might be better secured under some form of communism or other regulations of property. As a matter of fact, it was asserted that a communistic form of society preceded the institution of private property. Laveleye in Belgium, Sumner Maine in England and Friedrich Engels in Germany are among the major exponents of this theory. They had many disciples. But these men probably brought forth their ideas because they liked to indulge in generalizations or because such ideas fitted their social beliefs. Recent research reveals different facts. Documentary evidence is far too sketchy to permit the generalization that communism was characteristic of old primitive societies. Even contemporary primitive societies usually recognize some form of private property.

The collectivism in old Egypt, China and India indicates nothing to the contrary. These societies resulted from a long evolution, and we have no proof that they accepted complete collectivism in the earlier stages of their development. Besides, there is evidence that they accepted the institution of private property. As far as the early peoples of Europe are concerned, a number of historians reject the proposition that their societies were communistic. Although there existed certain forms of public ownership in Greece, private property also was recognized, and in all probability preceded public ownership. In Rome, private property was always recognized. The public land (*ager publicus*) never existed when private property was not also acknowledged. The former was permanently fed by conquests and constantly eaten up by the inroads of private property. The Gauls allowed for private property, as also did the Germanic tribes. Modern historical evidence suggests the type of ownership that is likely to be adopted under primitive conditions. In the French as well as in the English colonies in the New World, originally there was an extensive "no-man's-land" which was *res nullius* rather than *res communis*—nobody's, rather than everybody's, property. However, more and more plots of land became privately owned. It was only later that the state, becoming more firmly established in these virgin lands, seized some of the remaining no-man's-land and so-called public lands (*domaines publics*), which were nothing but interstices between sections of land which were privately owned. Thus private ownership preceded public ownership.

Whereas the importance of private property was recognized in primitive societies, there is no evidence that other rights of the individual enjoyed similar protection. An exception to the above is the right to the security of life. A person could not arbitrarily be deprived of his life. Procedures existed also for the protection of the individual's physical freedom. But such rights as freedom of religion and conscience, of speech, of assembly and association were not recognized. The fact that private property enjoyed a recognition which was granted only to the physical freedom and to the life of the individual indicates its importance.

The Importance of Property in More Advanced Societies

The relative importance of property is also evident in more advanced societies, and demonstrated by famous codes.

Whereas property rights were recognized as a major characteristic of our civilization, this acknowledgment is not prevalent in regard to other rights. The Decalogue is a case in point. It provides for the protection of life by commanding, "Thou shalt not kill," and it grants the same degree of protection of our belongings by ordering, "Thou shalt not steal." None of the other rights of men are mentioned. As a matter of fact, it is suggested that those rights might be rightfully restricted. The prohibition of apostasy and the statement that there is just one God amount to a denial of freedom of religion, a freedom considered by many the most important and fundamental of the individual's rights. The Decalogue's provisions appear to be symbolic. For the absence of freedom of religion seems to be as characteristic a feature of our civilization as the recognition of private property.

Greece is not famous for having championed religious liberty. In Rome, where private property enjoyed great protection, the early Christians were horribly persecuted. The Christian Church, which advocated private property, opposed religious freedom. Once Christianity became the religion of Rome, it withheld from heretics the liberty for which Christians of previous generations had fought. Augustine favored freedom of religion as long as heretics held a position of hegemony in Africa. Later, he attempted to consolidate orthodoxy. His doctrines became the foundation for persecutions in the name of Christianity.

Bluntschli remarked sarcastically that the Augustinian doctrine holds that when error prevails, it is right to invoke liberty of conscience, but when the truth predominates, it is just to use coercion. And the truth consisted in what the Church asserted to be true. Intolerance characterized the Middle Ages. In 1184, Emperor Frederick Barbarossa assured Pope Lucius III at Verona that the Church's attempts to preserve religious unity would have the support of the secular power. This agreement was supplemented by enactments in various countries during the centuries which followed. When St. Thomas and other scholastics stressed the value of private property, Popes Innocent III, Gregory IX and Innocent IV devised severe methods of religious persecution. When the Spanish doctors issued defenses of property, the Inquisition raged. Vitoria justified the *conquista* by claiming that the Indians would be forced to convert to the Catholic faith. Other nations experienced similar suppressions of religious freedom during the Reformation and Counter-Reformation. In Italy, Giordano Bruno and Galileo Galilei were martyred. The intolerance of the Catholic church did not change greatly in later days. As late as the nineteenth century, freedom of religion was opposed. Gregory XVI, in his encyclical *Mirari* of 1832, declared freedom of conscience in the lay sense to be nothing but the freedom to err. In 1864, Pius IX's *Quanta Cura* denounced freedom of religion as *libertatem perditionis*. It was condemned in the Syllabus of that year. Leo XIII, an advocate of private property in his encyclicals *Quod Apostoli Muneris* and *Rerum Novarum,* in *Libertas Protestantissimum* acknowledged freedom of speech, writing and instruction in religious matters only if it served the truth as conceived by the Roman church.

Nor did the Protestants, who also had advocated private property, favor religious tolerance. They were intolerant not only of Catholics. Their major groups, engaged in a life-and-death struggle with the Catholic church, counteracted internal tendencies that threatened disintegration, and imposed standards of conformism which were scarcely more flexible than those imposed by Rome. This occurred even in places where Protestant groups were not immediately challenged. In New England, for instance, the Puritans abandoned the idea of religious liberty, for which their ancestors had fought, in spite of the relative security from inimical churches. The intolerance of a Nathaniel Ward and a John Winthrop testify to this fact.

Even during the Enlightenment, when property rights received high sanction, freedom of religion, although it became more and more recognized, did not win general approval. Milton favored toleration for Protestant sects, but not for the more radical nonconformists and Catholics. The era's greatest defender of private property, John Locke, was not very enthusiastic about religious freedom. His *Letter Concerning Toleration,* frequently praised as a defense of religious freedom, is a qualified defense only. Locke claimed that liberty of conscience and of worship are natural rights. However, he excluded from the blessings of religious freedom people who professed politically subversive ideas or atheism, and thus opened the way for state intervention in ecclesiastical affairs. Rousseau's "civil religion" was as intolerant in form as that of the existing churches.

The attitude of Catholics, Protestants and enlightened thinkers was matched by the laws of temporal authorities. The Compromise of Augsburg of 1555, under which the subjects had to confess the religion of their rulers, was not abandoned for some time. The Edict of Nantes, issued by Henry IV of France in 1598 and granting freedom to the Huguenots, was revoked by Louis XIV of France in 1685. Although Elizabethan England permitted recusants to worship in private, they were deprived of certain rights. Later, in the seventeenth century, when religious animosities grew, the situation became worse. Dissident Protestants and Catholics were suspected, not only because their ideas conflicted with those of the Anglican church, but also because the anti-absolutist beliefs of the nonconformists and the papism of the Catholics were considered dangerous to the Stuart regime. Cromwell's constitution, while protecting property rights as well as securing freedom of worship for Protestant sects, still was intolerant of Catholics. The Declaration of Indulgence of 1672, although revealing a more conciliatory attitude toward Catholics, did not grant them full equality. Similarly, the Act of Toleration, issued by William III in 1689, discriminated against them. Other governments also were reluctant to recognize religious freedom. Joseph II of Austria permitted only limited rights of worship to the followers of the Augsburg and Helvetic confessions and the

Uniate Greek church in his Patent of Toleration. The Prussian Territorial Code of 1794 guaranteed equal privileges to the Lutheran, Reformed and Catholic churches, but withheld similar rights from other religious groups.

The Ten Commandments cannot be justly blamed for the religious intolerance throughout history. Although its provisions probably facilitated that intolerance, other factors also must have influenced it. If there had existed an urgent desire for religious freedom, then that freedom would have become established at an early stage. However, whereas the necessity for a protection of life and of property was recognized, that for freedom of religion was not acknowledged. Likewise, it would be unfair to blame the Decalogue for not mentioning other rights of the individual. On the other hand, that omission was not conducive to a future protection of these rights, since it seemed to imply their irrelevance or nonexistence. Yet, if there had existed an urgent need for the protection of such rights as freedom of speech or assembly, then they would have been recognized in the same way in which property rights were acknowledged. Furthermore, the Decalogue is not the only classic document that, while protecting life and property, did not command respect before other rights.

The situation is the same with regard to the classic English charter of liberty in the Middle Ages. The name *Magna Carta Libertorum*—great charter of liberties—should not suggest incorrect conclusions with respect to the actual content of the charter. Not by any means are all the rights of Englishmen mentioned in it. The veneration it later enjoyed provoked interpretations of its clauses which would have surprised the drafters. "Seventeenth century lawyers, ignorant of the law of the early 13th century, knowing nothing of the conditions of the time, saw in the charter a solemn grant to the people of England of rights which the Stuart kings were withholding. Trial by jury, the principle of habeas corpus, the right of parliament to control taxation, all these were thought to have been secured by Magna Carta. Even the great historians of the 19th century wrote of the charter with more enthusiasm than judgment." [1] Actually, neither the rights mentioned above, nor more modern rights, such

---

[1] Doris M. Stenton, "Magna Carta," *Encyclopaedia Britannica* (1958), XIV, 628.

as freedom of religion, speech, assembly or association, are listed in the charter. On the other hand, Magna Carta abounds with statements securing property rights. It provides that justice be done in the case of wrongful dispossessions by the monarch, and that illegal fines be remitted. No constable or bailiff is to take a man's corn or other chattels without immediate payment. No sheriff, bailiff or other person shall take a freeman's horses or carts for carriage duty. Neither the king nor his bailiffs are permitted to take a man's timber for castle-building or any other royal work. The land of the debtor is not to be seized if the debtor has sufficient chattels to pay the debt. The debtor's sureties are not to be distrained as long as the debtor himself can pay. If the sureties are called on they are to hold the debtor's land until their payment has been restored to them. No scutage or aid is to be taken without the matter being brought before the feudal council of tenants in chief, except for the ransoming of the king's body, the knighting of his eldest son or the first marriage of his eldest daughter. In view of all these recognitions of the rights of private property one is tempted to ask whether or not the provision of clause forty, "To no one will we sell, deny, or delay right or justice," primarily amounts to a protection of property rights. At any rate, the high rank assigned to these rights is obvious in clause thirty-nine: "No freeman shall be taken, or imprisoned, or disseised, or outlawed, or exiled or in any way destroyed, nor will we go upon him, nor will we send upon him, except by the legal judgment of his peers or by the law of the land." Property is valued as highly as life and physical freedom.

In spite of the fact that they both emphasized the protection of life and property and neglected other rights, the Ten Commandments and Magna Carta show differences which indicate an increasing recognition of human rights from antiquity to the Middle Ages. The Decalogue only mentions the rights of life and property. Magna Carta mentions many more. Although it omits several of the modern rights of Englishmen and emphasizes those of life and property, it protects many other rights. Thus freedom of movement is guaranteed and is extended to foreigners. It is provided that amercements are to be in proportion to the seriousness of the offense. In the case of grievous crimes, they are not to be so heavy that they deprive the offender of his means of livelihood. Writs of enquiry touching life or limb shall be granted freely. No one is to be arrested upon the appeal of a woman for the death of any other than her husband. The relatively greater appreciation of life and property in Magna Carta can probably be concluded from the fact that, in contrast to the framing of the Decalogue, these rights are described in greater detail. Although it may be debatable whether or not short commands like "Thou shalt not kill" or "Thou shalt not steal" are better guaranties of life and property than the wordy phrases of Magna Carta, it can, on the other hand, be argued that the detailed prescriptions of the English charter indicate that these rights were so generally accepted and were taken for granted to such a great extent that one could offer, instead of short, slogan-like phrases, more detailed descriptions of how these rights would be protected. Finally, the greater protection afforded to human rights by Magna Carta is evident in the fact that, whereas the Decalogue restricts an important right like freedom of religion, Magna Carta refrains from putting restrictions upon the rights it mentions.

The tendency toward a more comprehensive recognition of human rights continued after Magna Carta. In spite of the general atmosphere of intolerance, freedom of religion was by no means rejected by everyone. Maximus of Madaura had defended it at the time of Augustine. Marsilius of Padua, living shortly after Innocent III and Thomas Aquinas, favored it, as also did the monarchomarchs and Bodin at the time of the Inquisition. In the Netherlands, Grotius inspired the first edict of toleration that was promulgated by the States General in 1614. A hundred years later, Bayle published his important work on universal tolerance. In the meantime, the Arminian Baptists, headed by Hanserd Knollys, had promoted the idea of religious freedom in America. In 1644, Roger Williams had published *The Bloudy Tenant of Persecution* and, nineteen years later, Rhode Island had attained religious freedom. Similar tendencies could be observed in Europe throughout the seventeenth century. Protestant groups, or the governments influenced by them, had shown a great amount of intolerance. However, the Reformation stimulated the desire for freedom and, challenging religious orthodoxy, advanced the cause of religious liberty.

The increasing emancipation of men was not confined to the religious sphere. Freedom of speech and the press, for some time as severely restricted as freedom of religion, also became more and more recognized. Although the works of heterodox writers were proscribed by the Apostolic Constitutions and were opposed by the Council of Nicea; although indexes of prohibited books were issued by the papacy from 1559; although censorship was established, not only in the Catholic world, but also by temporal governments, yet there existed the desire for free speech and for freedom of the press. Finally, these rights were guaranteed by the governments of the various states. As one author said of freedom of speech and the press: "Milton anticipates it, but Locke, Voltaire, Rousseau, Wilkes, Paine, Camden, Erskine and Jefferson are of it, while Cobbett, Carlile and Mill carry on its issues." [2]

Besides freedom of speech and of the press, other rights were increasingly recognized and protected. Habeas corpus, freedom of assembly and any other particular rights—all of them were considered essential parts of human freedom. However, the acknowledgement of more and more parts of freedom did not impair the recognition of property rights. But the names of Milton and Locke, Voltaire and Rousseau, Jefferson and Paine suggest revolutions which played an important part in the emancipation of men. Therefore, we will now examine how property fared in relation to other liberal rights in these revolutions.

Property and Liberal Rights in the Democratic Revolutions

Private property was recognized as being at least equal to other liberal rights in the English, American and French revolutions.

Property is valued in the documents which resulted from the struggle against absolute monarchy in England, namely, the Petition of Right, the Instrument of Government and the Bill of Rights.

---

[2] J. M. Landis, "Freedom of Speech and of the Press," *Encyclopaedia of the Social Sciences*, VI, 456.

Significantly, the Petition of Right, drafted in 1628 under the guidance of Sir Edward Coke, quotes only that clause of Magna Carta that, more than any other provision of the famous charter, demonstrates the parity of property with life and liberty: "No freeman may be taken or imprisoned or be disseised of his freehold or liberties, or his free customs, or be outlawed or exiled, or in any manner destroyed, but by the lawful judgment of his peers, or by the law of the land." Illegal taxation is denounced at the beginning, and at the end of the enumeration of complaints the fact that people have been unjustly condemned and subsequently executed is mentioned. Thus the impairment of property and deprivation of life form the framework for the denunciation of the King's abuses. In the middle portions of this document, arbitrary imprisonment and the billeting of soldiers are criticized. The same order of enumeration is employed in the actual petition to the King: "That no man hereafter be compelled to make or yield any gift, loan, benevolence, tax or such like charge, without common consent by Act of Parliament; and that none be called to make answer, or take such oath, or to give attendance, or be confined, or otherwise molested or disquieted concerning the same, or for refusal thereof; and that no freeman, in any such manner as is beforementioned, be imprisoned or detained; and that your Majesty will be pleased to remove the said soldiers and mariners, and that your people may not be so burdened in time to come; and that the aforesaid commissions for proceeding by martial law, may be annulled; and that thereafter no commissions of like nature may issue forth to any person whatsoever, to be executed as aforesaid, lest by colour of them any of your Majesty's subjects be destroyed or put to death, contrary to the laws and franchise of the land."

Although in the 1640's the Puritan revolution resorted to bloodshed and abolished the monarchy, it did not oppose the institution of private property. Cromwell's Instrument of Government, issued in 1653, demonstrates that fact. The document assigns a superior position to property rights. Aside from property, only one right is mentioned, namely, freedom of religion. Although the latter is expanded for Protestants, it is considerably restricted for members of other confessions. On the other hand, even though article eighteen of the Instrument of Government established property qualifications for the right to vote, yet it does not restrict property rights. Article six prescribes that no tax, charge or imposition shall be laid upon the people without the consent of Parliament. Article thirty provides that money for the armed forces must be raised by Parliament. Article thirty-nine appears as a bulwark for vested rights. Since the Instrument of Government mentions only the right of property and that of religion, and since the latter right is restricted whereas the former is not, property rights seem to rank the highest among liberal rights.

In the Bill of Rights of 1689, property rights are considered equal to other rights. First, James II is accused of having endeavored to subvert and to extirpate the liberties of the English. Among such accusations as raising and keeping a standing army in time of peace without the consent of Parliament; quartering soldiers contrary to law; having prosecuted people in the Court of King's bench, for matters and causes cognizable only in Parliament; disarming Protestants; demanding excessive bail from persons committed in criminal cases and eluding the benefit of the laws for the liberty of the subjects; permitting excessive fines and illegal and cruel punishments, there can be found the accusation that the King arbitrarily infringed upon the property of his subjects "by levying money for and to the use of the Crown, by pretence of prerogative, for other time, and in other manner than the same was granted by Parliament." Property rights appear similarly in the latter part of the Bill, where the "ancient rights and liberties" of Englishmen are reaffirmed. Among clauses providing for more religious freedom and for the right of Protestants to bear arms, and prohibiting the raising and keeping of standing armies in time of peace and the requisition of excessive bail or the imposition of excessive fines or the infliction of cruel and unusual punishments, there can be found the provision "that levying money for or to the use of the Crown, by pretence or prerogative, without grant of Parliament, for longer time or in other manner than the same is or shall be granted, is illegal." At the end, the Commons pledge themselves to maintain their majesties "to the utmost of their powers, with their lives and estates."

The American Revolution, largely influenced by the Whig revolution, recognized the importance of property among liberal rights. This is evident in the Declaration of Independence, the bills of rights of the states and the Constitution.

Property rights occupy a prominent position in the Declaration of Independence. The "pursuit of happiness," meaning mainly the free acquisition, possession and use of property, is proclaimed as one of the inalienable rights of man at the very beginning of the Declaration, besides those of life and liberty. Even if one does not accept the idea that the pursuit of happiness means the protection of property, property rights still appear to be valued as equal to other rights. First, it could be claimed that they are included in that other inalienable right proclaimed at the outset—liberty. Obviously liberty, meaning the individual's general liberty, in the absence of specific exclusions, would embrace all the particular liberties of men, including the rights of property. Second, property rights are ranked on a par with other liberal rights in later passages. Thus the accusation that British officers harass the colonists is mentioned in the same breath as the complaint that these officers eat out the colonists' substance. The statement that British troops are not being punished for murdering Americans is followed by a note that the King extinguished the colonists' trade with other parts of the world. The complaint about the imposition of taxes without consent is followed by one about the deprivation of the benefits of trial by jury. The King "has plundered our seas, ravaged our coasts, burnt our towns, and destroyed the lives of our people" is written in another passage which indicates that property is considered as valuable as life itself. Finally, the very last sentence of the document states that the colonists pledge their lives, fortunes and honor to support the Declaration.

Occasionally, the Declaration of Independence is considered to favor the poor over the rich and a "fair" distribution of property rather than its protection. It is said that the statement "all men are created equal" elevates equality over freedom. However, this is hardly the case. "Life, liberty and the pursuit of happiness" are considered inalienable rights of man, while equality is not. The most significant principle of the Declaration is not equality, but freedom. And nowhere in this document can there be found any indication that the value of property is not equal to any of the particular liberties which the Declaration asserts.

The parity of property with other liberal rights is also evident in the bills of rights which were adopted by the new states. The classic example of Virginia is a case in point. In its first section, "the enjoyment of life and liberty, with the means of acquiring and possessing property," are proclaimed as inherent rights of men. Apart from this general statement, property rights are valued equally with other rights in the more specific clauses which follow. Section six provides that men "cannot be taxed or deprived of their property for public uses, without their own consent . . . nor bound by any law to which they have not, in like manner, assembled, for the public good." Laws which infringe upon property are considered as detrimental as laws which interfere with other rights! Under section eleven, trial by jury is prescribed, not only in criminal cases, but also "in controversies respecting property, and in suits between man and man."

Similar provisions can be found in the bills of rights which were adopted by other states. Also here, property ranks with liberty and life as an inherent right of man. Controversies over property enjoy the privilege of trial by jury. No less can a person be deprived of his property than can his life or liberty be taken away from him. Property is as secure from search and seizure as the person is. Every member of society is entitled to enjoy his property as much as his life and liberty.

The equality of private property with other liberal rights thus is evident in the wording of specific articles. However, the fact that these articles are just a few among many other provisions securing various liberties, such as freedom of religion, speech, the press, also demonstrates the truth of this assertion. The bills of rights do not suggest that property rights are inferior to these liberties. The egalitarian character which frequently has been attributed to the early state constitutions is not present in their bills of rights.

Finally, property appears as an important right in the Constitution of the United States, a right that is definitely on a par with, if not superior to, other liberal rights. Although the word "property" is not expressly mentioned in the preamble, nevertheless the protection of property is included in the statement regarding the aims of the people. The assertion that the Constitution is ordained and established to secure the blessings of liberty implies that property should be protected, for "liberty" is a general concept and includes all particular liberties which are not specifically exempted. It includes property rights. The intent of the framers to protect property in the preamble can be concluded also from the declaration that a more perfect union is formed in order to establish justice and insure domestic tranquility, since these values, at the time at which the Constitution was framed, were threatened mainly by actions which were endangering property rights.

The protection of property can be seen also in the articles of the Constitution. Section nine of article one, besides providing for the writ of habeas corpus and prohibiting bills of attainder and *ex post facto* laws, prohibits arbitrary tax laws. The following section is even more outspoken. Keeping the states from passing bills of attainder and *ex post facto* laws, it prohibits also, due to infringements upon property through state legislation, the passage of laws impairing the obligation of contracts.

Finally, property, like such rights as freedom of religion, speech, the press and of assembly as well as the right to keep and bear arms and to be free from cruel and unusual punishment, is protected in the amendments of the Constitution. Following the pattern set by some of the states, the United States Bill of Rights grants under the fourth amendment the same degree of protection from search and seizure to property as it does to the person of the individual. The right of trial by jury is not only guaranteed for criminal prosecutions, but also for suits at common law which involve property. The fifth amendment, besides making provision for indictment by grand jury, and guaranteeing protection against double jeopardy and self-incrimination, states that no person shall "be deprived of life, liberty or property, without due process of law." Later, this "due process clause" was made applicable to the states in the fourteenth amendment.

While there can be no doubt that throughout the Constitution property rights are valued as highly as other liberal rights, it could be argued that they were even dearer to the framers than were such rights as freedom of religion, speech and assembly and other liberties mentioned in amendments, because their protection was already provided for in the original text of the Constitution.

THE PROPERTY BASE OF CAPITALISM
—
By John Chamberlain*

THE market, which is the characteristic institution of capitalism, expresses a relationship of buyer and seller. It is, in effect, what, results when free choice is applied to the disposition of property—or of what is made with the use of property—by "mixing" labor with it. The comparisons which the market permits lead to the creation of value, which is a compromise of individual judgments. The seller seeks to cover the labor and energy he has expended, plus a profit; the buyer seeks to save himself labor and energy by making an exchange. Two subjectivities meet in an objective price. But behind the creation of value there must be ownership—the right to dispose of a good or a service.

So we come back to property as the base for liberty. In *Wealth of Nations,* which is the first good book about the market, Adam Smith had plenty to say about free choice, about the simple system of natural liberty. But, like other economists of an older day, he tended to assume the property right. This right, in the pages of Smith, is something which is anterior to economics as such. Where property could not be freely traded he expressed his displeasure; witness his attacks on primogeniture and entail, those laws which kept much of the land of England and Scotland from coming freely on the market. But, in spite of the feudal hobbles which still existed in his day, Adam Smith took private ownership for granted. In doing this he was exercising his pre-

* John Rensselaer Chamberlain received his Ph.D. from Yale University in 1925. From 1926 to 1928 he was a reporter for the *New York Times.* He was editor of *Life Magazine* 1945–50 and of the *Freeman* 1950–52. He was an associate editor of *Barron's Magazine* from 1953 to 1955 and then a staff writer on the *Wall Street Journal* and a daily columnist for the King Features Syndicate in New York.

His writings include *Farewell to Reform* (1932), *The Enterprising Americans* (1959) and *A Business History of the United States* (1963).

The selection below is from *The Roots of Capitalism* (1959). It is reprinted by permission of D. Van Nostrand Co., Inc.

rogatives as a free-born British subject. But it was not until Smith's own time that Englishmen could take the property right for granted. That right had been bitterly contested in most previous generations, though usually in its political rather than in its more purely economic aspects.

Whether a discussion of "rights," either "natural" or legal, belongs to a book on economics is an arguable point. But "rights" have their important effect on the flow of human energy, and therefore on the creation of the wealth that reaches the marketplace for valuation in exchange. It is not much to say that economics could not exist at all without the prior establishment of the rights to life, liberty and property—or, in the older word, "estate."

The "right" to life must be assumed if the race itself is not to perish: without it, human existence would indeed be "nasty, brutish and short" and only a few consummately clever murderers would soon be left to people the earth. The other rights of the famous triad can be deduced from the first: if one has a "right" to life, one must be at liberty to work and sustain oneself, and one must have access to the means of production, specifically land and tools. If one can be legally deprived of the rights to acquire these, the right to life becomes a permission to be revoked at the politician's or the military man's will.

From the standpoint of economics, the three basic rights are necessary if there is to be any economic calculation. Under slave systems, or under the "planned" disposition of energy and goods that is part and parcel of any permissive system, the market simply ceases to function. Under planning one takes what one gets according to a superior's definition of good, and there's an end to it. Pricing is done by the whim or guess of the patriarch or the planner, without relation to the desires of buyer and seller, and the measurement of value thus becomes an impossibility. Without a method of measurement, of registering the comparative force of human desires, economics as a science must cease to exist.

In recent years, forgetting that the three rights are indissolubly linked (indeed, they are three faces of the same thing), fashionably smart people have fallen into the habit of opposing "human rights" to "property rights." Jefferson (or Franklin

Roosevelt) stood for "humanity" where Hamilton (or Hoover) stood for property; therefore, down with Hamilton (or Hoover)! But, despite the fashionable notion, the property right is just as much a human right as any other. Where there is no property right, human beings are invariably kicked around—by the politicians, as in Soviet Russia; by the military, as in any War Lord system; or by a priestcraft, as in Peru of the Incas.

Englishmen knew this both instinctively and from experience long before Adam Smith first listened to Francis Hutcheson on the subject of natural liberty. In the days of the barons, when property relations were regulated by a grand permissive system which envisioned the king (with his Divine Right) as the chief feudal holder and all others his vassals, there may have been no abstract "property right" in land. But if permissiveness governed all things in 1215, the year of Magna Carta, the barons who exacted the Great Charter from bad King John on the meadow at Runnymede were hardly disposed to admit it. With them, permissiveness had become prescription. They assumed that the land was theirs in exchange for the performance of duties (the chief taxes of the time). Much of Magna Carta is taken up with such things as the rights of heirs living under guardians, and the rights of debtors against bailiffs who would seize lands or rents without regard to the debtors' net worth in chattels. Prescriptive property rights, indeed, are the substance of Magna Carta, and the protection of these rights is pushed backward toward the protection of persons and forward again into the protection of the conditions or channels of trade. Thus, the indissolubility of life, liberty, and property was recognized even as early as at the very start of the thirteenth century.

Under Magna Carta no freeman could be deprived of his freehold except by the "law of the land." All merchants were guaranteed safe and secure entry to or exit from England, with the right to tarry there and to buy and sell "quit from all evil tolls." Sheriffs and bailiffs were forbidden to take the carts or horses of freemen for transport duty, or wood which was not theirs, or "corn or other provisions . . . without immediately tendering money therefor." Fines and "amercements" imposed against the "law of the land" were to be remitted; Welshmen "disseised" of lands or liberties were to have their property or rights restored to them; and the "men in our kingdom" were to "have and hold all the aforesaid liberties, rights and concessions (of Magna Carta) well and peaceably, freely and quietly, fully and wholly, for themselves and their heirs, in all respects and in all places, forever, as is aforesaid."

If all this was merely "barons' justice," as has been frequently charged by those who try to make it seem that the common man had no rights in medieval England, then the barons of King John's time (or the churchmen who stood behind them) were extraordinarily sympathetic men. True, the villeins on their estates, the serfs who were bound to the soil, were not to achieve freedom for some time to come (either by deserting to the towns or by making individual deals with the landlord when labor became scarce after the Black Death). Nevertheless, the justice which the barons demanded for themselves was applicable to many others. The barons asked for reasonable fines, proportioned to the offense; for justice as a right, "not to be sold, denied or delayed"; for security of person as well as property; for uniform weights and measures; for freedom of travel; for a redress of church grievances and, in general, for a recognition of common law rights as the "law of the land." All this was applicable across the board—and twelfth-century "Anglo-Saxon writ" and thirteenth-century "Anglo-Norman writ-charter" thus became the basis of "the immemorial rights of Englishmen" which were the colonists' quite legitimate concern at the outset of the American Revolution.

The struggle for the property right was always a checkered one in the ages when the divine right theory sanctioned the king as the feudal overlord of all land owners. Nevertheless, Magna Carta was confirmed under Edward I, with a kingly admission that no seizures of goods would be made for the crown's use; and all through the later Middle Ages judges applied the rights of the Great Charter as the "law of the land." The king, ideally, was supposed to be "under God and the law."

In France, where anyone could be imprisoned if the king chose to sign a letter of arrest bearing the privy seal, there was no such safety of life, liberty and property as in England. Whether the English dispensation came "out of the German forests" (the old-time Angles and Saxons thought of law as a quest for the Creator's justice) or from the Roman Stoic philosophers who had elaborated the concept of "natural," or ideal, law is immaterial to the fact that Englishmen, from their twelfth- and thirteenth-century beginnings, held that rights came with birth and not from any permissive act of king or State. The Common Law was there before the king, for it originated in man's intuitive recognition of rules of conduct that were suited to the nature of man.

The Tudors broke with the theory of the thirteenth century by seizing the properties of the monasteries and distributing them among their handymen and court retainers. This lawless act not only put the property right in question, but it also saddled the State with the necessity of caring for the indigent and the aged who had hitherto been supported by the contributions of churchmen. True enough, Queen Elizabeth had the native good sense to refrain from pushing her assumed prerogatives too far, and adventurous Englishmen began acquiring wealth and property from all over the globe during her reign. Even so, the temperamental Elizabeth insisted on infringing the property right by granting trade monopolies to her favorites. Though she allowed the courts to speak their piece, it was more or less in vain that defendants cited Magna Carta in her later years to prove that any freeman of the town might buy and sell "all things merchantable in London."

So things stood at the onset of the seventeenth century, when the Stuarts came in to assert the divine right theory even more forcibly than Elizabeth. This was the century when the courts (as championed by the doughty Chief Justice Coke) came to the "crunch of war" with the crown. Edward Coke, in his several activities as judge, member of parliament, and commentator on Magna Carta, provided most of the groundwork for American constitutional law by his insistence that no one could be deprived of rights without full and fair hearing or in consonance with stated government powers. Coke's importance to economics resides in his clarification of the old English guarantees that no one can be ousted from a freehold or deprived of a livelihood without due process of law. The economic aspects of Coke's thinking were put on high ground by his assertion that monopolies and impositions on trade come under the heading of deprivations of liberty. Thus, once again liberty and property rights were accepted on high legal authority as being facets of the same thing.

The seventeenth century also saw parliament (the focus of the forces making the Puritan Revolution) siding with the courts in the battle which finally established the "separation of the powers" as the physical guarantee that no executive authority could ride roughshod over the "immemorial rights of Englishmen." The Puritan Revolution was not fought over mundane things, for it was, in the bright dawn before the new "presbyters" became as intolerant as John Milton's "old priests," a struggle for the right of the individual to read the Bible for himself and to dissent in religious matters if he so pleased. However, the "property right" was deeply involved in the fight on all levels. First of all, the Puritans who objected to being forced to abide by the spiritual decisions of the Church of England also disliked paying the king "ship money" (a seizure of property) without parliamentary representation in tax matters. Hampden, whose personal assessment of ship money was a mere twenty shillings, brought the matter into court on the ground of libertarian principle, and the battle was joined. The Roundhead, or parliamentary, party saw clearly that all the immemorial rights of Englishmen were indissolubly linked in the struggle against the arbitrariness of the king.

Cromwell's army was an army of pamphleteers, and it had its individualist and primitive communist wings. The Levellers (not really Levellers, for they believed in the natural inequality that arises from the vast variety of human abilities) spoke for ancient rights which had been affirmed by Coke and championed by Hampden in the ship money case. The Diggers, who got their name because they insisted on squatting and "digging" to plant parsnips and beans where they pleased, were land communists. Their chief spokesman, Gerrard Winstanley, said equivocally: "Property there must be, but all must possess it." With the property right thus under attack from the two extremes of the political spectrum, the Stuart kings at one end and the Winstanley Digger Puritans at the other, it is scarcely cause for wonder that Englishmen began to think more clearly than ever before about the relation of private property to both the physical and spiritual needs of man. The result of the intellectual churning of the seventeenth-century struggle was some twenty thousand tracts—and two great works bearing on the property right and government, Thomas Hobbes's *Leviathan* and John Locke's *Second Treatise on Civil Government.*

In the conflicts and in the single basic agreement of Hobbes and Locke, the meaning of the seventeenth century comes clear. Hobbes was the older man: he was born in 1588, the year of the defeat of the Spanish Armada, and he died at the venerable age of 91, long after the restoration of the Stuarts. Like the Calvinists, Hobbes believed in the sinful nature of man—in a state of nature, he said, it is "every man against every man," and life, in consequence, is "solitary, poor, nasty, brutish and short." In his shrewd guess that there had never been a "golden age" of primitive freedom, Hobbes, who had not had the benefit of modern anthropological research, rested his case on pure assumption. But it was a reasonable enough inference at a time when Oliver Cromwell's rule and that of his incompetent son, "Tumbledown Dick," was going to pieces. If men were "sociable one with another," said Hobbes, "like bees and ants," they would not need an "artificial covenant" to bind themselves to sociability. But, unlike the bees and the ants, men are "continually in competition for Honour and Dignity . . . and consequently amongst men there ariseth on that ground, Envy and Hatred, and finally Warre. . . ."

Nor could the individual conscience, as disciplined by religion, prevent that "warre." After all, it was over religious differences as well as over tax matters and parliamentary supremacy that the rebellion of the seventh century had been fought. Hobbes distrusted Puritans, he distrusted Quakers, he distrusted Catholics—or any "boy or wench (who) thought he spoke with God Almighty." To keep the peace, said Hobbes, a strong "artificiall" creature, a "great Leviathan," was necessary. Hobbes considered that the Leviathan "must have the power to overrule the individual judgment of men on all issues, whether of property or anything else." He was a totalitarian in all save one very English thing: he believed that government derived from a compact, or a contract, made between men to accept a ruler over them. Implied in the bond of this compact was the promise that the ruler would be just. Government was not accepted by men for the exaltation of the ruler, or for the mystical adoration of the State; it was accepted to obtain peace and protection in one's own estate.

As Hobbes put it, the "liberty of the subject . . . lyeth . . . in those things, which in regulating their actions, the Sovereign hath pratermitted: such as liberty to buy, and sell, and otherwise contract with one another; to choose their own aboad, their own diet, their own trade of life, and institute their children as they themselves think fit. . . ." And "the obligation of subjects to the sovereign is understood to last as long, and no longer, than the power lasteth, by which he is able to protect them. For the right men have by Nature to protect themselves, when none else can protect them, can by no covenant be relinquished. . . . The end of Obedience is Protection. . . ."

In other words, a *quid* for a *quo*. Both in his trust in a ruler's "protective" benevolence and in his feeling that the ruler would naturally "pratermit" the liberty to buy and sell, to live where one chose, and to bring up one's children in one's own way, Hobbes took great chances. He had been a tutor in mathematics to Charles II before the Restoration, and he thus knew the Stuarts at a time when they were willing to promise much in order to regain the Crown. Though he did not believe in divine right, his doctrine, which he presented in vellum to Charles II in exile, was good enough for a restoration-minded king. For had not Hobbes said that it was a "disease" of a "commonwealth" to believe "that he that hath the soveraigne power is subject to the civil lawes"? The Hobbesian compact gave total power to the king by free gift—and it was only another manifestation of "disease" to think the power could be "divided" into parliamentary, executive, and judicial compartments, each constituting a check on the other.

John Locke, whose phrases were to become the language of the American Revolution and the Declaration of Independence, was fully as disgusted as Hobbes with the excesses of the Puritan Commonwealth. Even as much as John Milton he came to think that "new Presbyter is but old priest writ large." But he did not react to the intolerance of the Cromwellian "liberators" with the extreme veneration for kingship that is implicit in Hobbes'

Leviathan. Possessing a supple and sinuous mind, with a scientist's insistence on precision (he was a physician as well as a philosopher), Locke was ultimately to show how a "compact" for a "soveraigne" could be made a two-way instrument, hedging the king about with agreed-upon limitations of the ruler's own liberties, and giving parliament a most effective veto on the executive through control over the power of the purse.

Locke was born in 1632, forty-four years after Hobbes, and he was only nine years old when the great Civil War of the seventeenth century broke out. His father, a fervent adherent of the Puritan cause, captained a Roundhead band in the west of England, where the seafarers of Bristol were up in arms about the ship money exactions. Locke himself had a strict Puritan upbringing, spending six years at Westminster School in London where he was surrounded by the tumult and the rumblings which led up to the beheading of Charles I. He went on to Christ Church at Oxford when that royalist institution was officially being "cleansed" by the Puritan party. But John Owen, the Dean of Christ Church, was a most tolerant Puritan at heart, and the spirit of toleration survived throughout Oxford as a whole during the entire Commonwealth period. The local Puritans permitted great scholars such as Dr. Edward Pococke, who taught Hebrew and Arabic to Locke, to remain at the university without taking the oath of allegiance to Cromwell. Locke's friends at Christ Church included unrepentant Royalists. It was from John Owen, the latitudinarian Puritan, that Locke in all probability picked up his key thought on toleration—that it is the duty of the State to let all religious sects alone except those whose aim is the subversion of the civil power.

By the time of the Stuart restoration Locke had pretty well lost his Puritanism. He welcomed the Restoration for its "quiet settlement," and hoped that men would be "kind to their religion, their country and themselves" by foregoing the "overzealous contention" of the Puritans. The "popular asserters of public liberty," he wrote, "are the greatest engrossers of it too." Continuing in this vein of subdued contrition, he said: "A general freedom is but a general bondage; . . . all the freedom I can wish my country or myself is, to enjoy the protection of those laws which the prudence and providence of our ancestors established, and the happy return of his majesty has restored."

But if, like Hobbes, he trusted the Stuarts to be protectors of ancestral liberties, he was soon to suffer the second disillusioning experience of his young life: Charles II soon broke his word and permitted a revival of ecclesiastical tyranny. By 1667 Locke's departure from Hobbesian thinking was clear. In an early essay on toleration (not to be confused with the more famous *Letter on Toleration* which he wrote in exile in 1685), the whole theory of the proper limitation of the respective spheres of individual and governmental action is stated with admirable precision.

Like Hobbes, Locke begins in 1667 with the idea that governments are necessary to "preserve men in this world from the fraud and violence of one another." This is the seventeenth-century view of human nature, and nothing that has happened in the twentieth has done much to disprove it. But since men remain men even when they are governors, it does not do to take any ruler on trust. Some method must be found to guard the guardians; and to keep "magistrates" from going out of bounds it must be clearly understood that they have no rule but the limited one of protecting men in their lives, their liberty, and their "estate."

Since the rise of Marxian criticism in the nineteenth century, it has become the fashion to say that the Glorious Revolution of 1688, which unseated James II and brought William of Orange to the throne of England, was the work of property holders who were totally uninterested in the larger question of the rights of everybody in the community. But the view of Locke was that if the State would stick to the narrow issue of preserving "life, liberty and estate" against the violence of thieves, anarchs and outside marauders, freedom and tolerance in all spheres would follow as a matter of course.

A government, said Locke in 1667, if derived from the people, can only have the power necessary to "their own preservation." "This being premised," he continued, ". . . the magistrate ought to do or meddle with nothing *but barely* in order to secure the civil peace and property of his subjects." The business of government was to make as few laws as possible; there was no need for "laws to any other end but only for the security of the government and protection of people in their lives, estates and liberties. . . ." And, so Locke asked in a bit of ringing rhetoric in defense of the religious tolerance which was his real overmastering concern, "can it be reasonable that he that cannot compel me to buy a house should force me his way to venture the purchase of heaven?"

In sum, Locke asserted that if a government began using force for any reason besides protecting individuals in their lives, liberties and estates against the presumption of force exerted by others, it thereby demeaned itself and no longer deserved to hold the allegiance of men. This amounted to a qualified right of revolution any time a government denied such things as freedom of speech, assembly and religion.[1] With Locke, toleration came first; the defense of property was the means to an end that could well be left to the individual without the intercession of government. Locke was property-minded because he was freedom-minded, not because he cared particularly for the material goods of this world as such.

All of Locke's basic distinctions were set down a full generation before the Glorious Revolution of 1688. They were set down in vivid recollection of the arbitrary compulsions in all spheres, whether religious, cultural or economic, of both the early Stuart regimes and the Cromwellian interlude. They were set down before Locke, as physician and tutor in the family of Anthony Ashley Cooper (or Lord Ashley), was drawn into a broad enterprise of his patron for colonizing the Carolinas. Locke served as secretary for Lord Ashley's colonizing group: he recorded the proposed constitution for the Carolinas in his own handwriting, and he is almost certainly the author of that part of the constitution which insisted on freedom for any religious sect which could muster as many as seven adherents.

The sole limitation to be placed on any "religion of seven" was that the liberties claimed by it should not include the liberty of attempting to coerce others to its beliefs. Applied to the

---

[1] Bertrand de Jouvenel and Willmoore Kendall observe that Locke provided for no defense against a possible "tyranny of the majority." His doctrine of parliamentary supremacy would allow a majority vote to "conclude the rest." But when Locke was writing, the House of Lords and the King's veto, to say nothing of the courts, constituted a check on pure majoritarianism. And in any event, Locke insisted the realm of "Caesar" did not include either religious teaching or economic decision.

modern day, Locke's "model" for a constitution would permit any party to exist that did not have for its aim the supercession or suppression of other parties. Clearly he would outlaw the Communist party as long as it adhered to its belief in the necessity of a dictatorship. But for all groups which believed in freedom he would say to government: "Hands off!"

Twenty-odd years after his part in writing the Fundamental Constitution of the Carolinas, Locke published his systematic presentations of ideas on toleration and the limited role of government. Although he had set forth his matured views on government as early as 1681, when he wrote them down for his own guidance, he withheld them until the final overthrow of the Stuarts made it safe to issue them. In the fashion that was increasingly to be followed by eighteenth-century thinkers, he ignored journalistic immediacy in favor of going back to first principles.

"In the beginning and first peopling of the great common of the world," he wrote in his famous *Second Treatise on Civil Government,*" . . . the law man was under was . . . for appropriating. God commanded, and his wants forced him, to labour. That was his property, which could not be taken from him wherever he had fixed it. And hence subduing or cultivating the earth, and having dominion, we see are joined together. The one gave title to the other. So that God, by commanding to subdue, gave authority so far to appropriate. And the condition of human life, which requires labour and materials to work on, necessarily introduces private possessions."

In the beginning, as anthropologists were later to surmise, "private possessions" were held in common by blood relations, the gens—or the house—of Roman antiquity, the ramified family clan which has persisted into modern times in the Scottish Highlands or the Indian village community. The conveyance of family-held lands to others could not be undertaken without the permission of all members of the clan. But if Locke—and Hobbes before him—knew nothing of anthropology, it still followed that labor, when "mixed" with raw materials, creates the original property right.

Following on from this, Locke argued that man must have a right to defend his own possessions and to bequeath or otherwise bestow them as he sees fit. But, since men are not angels, private judgment could not be relied upon to settle conflicting claims. "All private judgment of every particular member being excluded," said Locke, "the community comes to be the umpire; . . . those who are united unto one body, and have a common established law and judicature to appeal to, with authorities to decide controversies between them and punish offenders, are in civil society one with another. . . ." The society, of course, derives from the consent of the governed, and civil government "relates only to men's civil interests, is confined to the care of the things of this world, and hath nothing to do with the world to come; . . . the business of laws is not to provide for the truth of opinion, but for the safety and security of the commonwealth, and of every particular man's goods and person."

Again and again Locke hammered it home, both in the *Second Treatise on Civil Government* and in the *Letter on Toleration,* that the "political society is instituted for no other end, but only to secure every man's possessions of the things of this life." The soul, the things of the spirit, and the transmission of possessions in the marketplace were "not to be compelled . . . either by law or force."

Before Locke, people had tended to confuse the concept of "society" with the concept of the State. Where Locke was a distinct advance on Hobbes—or on Aristotle, for that matter—was in his feeling that society and the State are two distinct things. The function of the State is to permit people to live in society by protecting them in their property relationships, and to keep them from killing, maiming, or otherwise harming each other. But beyond that both individuals and society are to be left alone to order things by mutual contract or by the principle of voluntary association. The whole realm of governmental interference with economic matters—whether it concerns the fixing of prices, or the "planning" of industry, or the seizure of one man's substance to endow another—becomes, in the Lockean view of things, an invasion of the social individual's right to do his own planning and association or to undertake his own bequests or charities.

Locke's was the theory of the umpire as against the vampire state, and in distant America, where the colonists followed English doings with an avidity that was only intensified by the time it took to get news of the homeland, his ideas were read and pondered along with Coke's commentary on Magna Carta, and Blackstone's later eighteenth-century commentaries on the law of England. The Lockean distinctions and Coke's teachings about the "law of the land" lay around like so much dry tinder, awaiting the spark that would be struck when the Hanoverian kings, forgetting that their patents to the Crown derived from the Whig tradition of 1688, tried to revive the pretentions of the Stuarts to absolute rule.

Private property, as Russell Kirk has said, has been a powerful instrument for teaching men and women responsibility, and for giving them the leisure to think and freedom to act with prudence. In the America which read Locke and Coke, property was the rule rather than the exception: as Gouverneur Morris was to point out at the time of the Constitutional Convention of 1787, some ninety percent of the colonists were members of freeholders' families. They were used to thinking for themselves and exercising their own responsibilities.

They had, indeed, been Lockean men from the beginning: America had come into being by Lockean social compacts, such as the Mayflower Compact, which instituted governments by popular consent. The colonists frequently departed from Lockean toleration, notably in the witch-burnings at Salem and in the persecutions that drove Roger Williams from Massachusetts Bay to Rhode Island and Hooker's charges to Hartford in the Connecticut valley. But the colonists, for all their moral frailties when it came to practicing what they preached, were accustomed to the distinction between society and the State, for their own Pilgrim or Quaker or Maryland Catholic (or even Cavalier) societies in the Old World had reacted to State persecution by emigration. As Trevelyan has put it, "twenty thousand Puritans had already carried their skill and industry, their silver and gold, their strivings and hopes" to the New World before the successful outcome of the Civil War revived hopes for their independent kind in England.

Naturally, the men who had dared to emigrate were attuned to Locke's thinking and quite ready to make it the "party line" of the American rebellion against George III. The Hanoverian kings' "plan" for seaboard.America—to keep it a raw-material country, to force it to buy tea from the East India Company's monopoly and manufactures from British merchants, and to seal it off from the Mississippi Valley, which was envisioned as a preserve for the fur trade with headquarters in Quebec— seemed to the Lockean colonists to be a complete invasion of everything that had been fought for in the English revolutions of the seventeenth century.

As for the non-Puritan sections of seaboard America, they had the Lockean tradition of tolerance as set forth in the Carolina constitution. The lawyers in these sections had also been reared on Coke's and Blackstone's commentaries, which insisted on the common-law rights of all Englishmen, regardless of where or in what status of life they might be. Jefferson and Washington spoke Locke's language even as John Adams in Massachusetts; moreover, though they had an obvious interest in the lands of the Ohio valley, they spoke it from more truly disinterested motives. After all, even though they groused at being in debt to British merchants, it would not have mattered so much to tobacco planters to be forced to remain in "raw material" status as producers, for their big market for tobacco was in England.

When Thomas Jefferson, a truly disinterested Virginian, repaired to his room in the bricklayer's house in Philadelphia to write the Declaration of Independence, his mind was full of the Lockean phrases. It was also full of rage against George III. The general principles of the Declaration—that men have inalienable rights to life, liberty and the pursuit of happiness (a Jefferson substitution which was by no means designed to subvert the property right)—were followed by a Lockean affirmation that governments are instituted by men to "secure these rights." Then came the full force of Jefferson's rage: George III was accused of a whole category of abuses, of "refusing" to assent to "wholesome and necessary" laws, of bribing judges, of rendering the military superior to the civil power, of quartering troops in colonists' homes, of cutting off the colonists' trade, of imposing taxes without consent, of depriving Americans of trial by jury, of plundering the seas and sending foreign mercenaries to "compleat the work of death, desolation and tyranny" and of suspending colonial legislatures and taking away colonial charters.

The rage behind Jefferson's short, stabbing phrases was real, but the form it took was an imitation that must have been artfully calculated to stress the relation of Anglo-Americans to English tradition. For Jefferson's bill of complaints follows the pattern of the complaints set forth in the English Bill of Rights of 1689, which was inspired by the thinking of Locke. Like the Declaration, the English Bill of Rights punched out a list of grievances in short, pithy sentences. King James II had "endeavored to subvert laws and liberties," he had levied money for Crown use without permission of parliament, he had quartered troops "contrary to law," he had disarmed Protestants at a time when "Papists were . . . armed," he had violated the freedom of parliamentary elections, he had imposed excessive fines and illegal and cruel punishments, and so forth and so on. The whole list, with minor changes, had found its echo in the Declaration of Independence almost a century later.

When he was accused by his fellow Virginians and by morose New Englanders of copying Locke and stealing from George Mason's Virginia Declaration of Rights, Jefferson answered that he "did not consider it as any part of my charge to invent new ideas." All he knew was that he "turned to neither book nor pamphlet while writing it." It was "intended as an expression of the American mind." The ideas were in the air, they had been thoroughly debated everywhere throughout the colonies, and even after the hacking process of editing the Declaration was ended, the words stood for the bold consensus of an embattled people.

Whether the sole original substitution in the Declaration—that of "pursuit of happiness" for "property"—was a wise substitution has often been argued. However, the violation of the Lockean triad hardly matters if one looks into the furnishings of Jefferson's own mind for a clue to his intention. No one can deny that "pursuit of happiness" is an inalienable right of the individual. (No one can pursue happiness for another, and no one can benefit by trying to steal the "pursuit" from somebody else.) Moreover, no one can "pursue happiness" for himself without paying some attention to "property" as a means to the end of contentment and enjoyment of one's days. Jefferson had no animus against property in speaking for happiness; he merely wished to use an idea that would make the blood race a little faster.

Indeed, Jefferson's reading in the 1770's included, besides Locke, a number of works which inquired specifically into the origins of property. Jefferson was fond of quoting from Lord Kames's *History of Property,* a book which argued that if men did not devote at least some time to their own estate, then "independency" and "liberty" would both be destroyed. With Jefferson both "independency" and "liberty" were absolutely necessary to the "pursuit of happiness." Again we come back to the indissoluble nature of all the "rights": life, liberty, property and the pursuit of happiness are all component parts of one great chain.

In any event, the colonists fought for "life, liberty and property" and eschewed happiness for the moment. When the long struggle was over at Yorktown, they returned to their property bases in the respective states. They soon found that neither life nor liberty could be sustained, or happiness pursued, without a special type of government which would guarantee respect for contractual relations among property holders who wished to trade in a single currency across state lines. So came the call for still another Lockean compact, the one that was to be hammered out at Philadelphia in 1787 by men who had read the *Second Treatise on Civil Government* and were bent on restating it in American terms.

Because the property right was protected in our basic document, free capitalism had the political climate it needed for expansion. Five years after the making of the Constitution, Hamilton's (and Tench Coxe's) famous report on manufactures noted the existence of an American steel industry, a flourishing shipbuilding industry and a copper and brass industry. The textile industry burgeoned quickly on these shores once Samuel Slater had slipped out of Britain with the blueprint of an Arkwright factory committed to memory. Protected by the limitation of government, and with the space of a continent in which to grow, the simple system of natural liberty had found its habitat. It was not to be seriously challenged for a hundred and fifty years.

PROPERTY

—

By Henry C. Wallich*

SQUARELY across the path of equality lies property. Private property is the classical symbol of economic inequality. Fundamental attacks upon inequality have traditionally taken the form of attacks on property. The defense of property has served, in large measure, as a justification also of economic inequality in a broader sense.

I shall argue that this roadblock today is assuming the form of a red herring. Property is not what it used to be. It is no longer the main source of inequality of income. Nor is it limited in total amount, as it was when land represented the principal form of income-producing property. This takes some of the edge off the question of why some people happen to own property and others do not.

The issue of property has agitated society since the dawn of civilization. Property never has ceased to be under atack. History is full of movements to share the other fellow's wealth, since the days when Solon annulled the debts of the Atheneans and when the Jewish Jubilee Year brought relief to debtors every fifty years. In response, immense ingenuity and effort have been called forth to organize property's defenses—legal, political and intellectual. Our attention here must focus upon the intellectual side of the battle.

Natural law naturally has been invoked on behalf of private

* Henry Christopher Wallich, economist and educator, came to the United States in 1935 from Germany. He received his M.A. from Harvard University in 1941 and his Ph.D. in 1944. In 1951 he became professor of economics at Yale, and in 1958 was named assistant to the secretary of the treasury. Wallich was appointed a member of the President's Council of Economic Advisers in 1959–60. He holds memberships in the American Economic Association and the American Finance Association.
   Monetary Problems of an Export Economy (1950) and *Public Finances of a Developing Country* (1951, with John Adler) are two of his works.
   The following selection is a chapter from *The Cost of Freedom* (1960), reprinted by permission of Harper &. Bros.

property as it has for so many other institutions whose justification is not immediately obvious. Strenuous efforts have been made to elevate property rights to the level of human rights—to a par with freedom and equality. But somehow property rights have never quite succeeded in establishing themselves at this lofty height. Perhaps they were held back by the weakness of the case, or perhaps by an uneasiness on the part of the sponsors that could conceivably be explained even without recourse to the Freudian interpretation of wealth. Consequently, the Declaration of Independence speaks of the pursuit of happiness, instead of the pursuit of property.

John Locke, to whom we are indebted for so much of our political philosophy, sought to strengthen the natural law argument by relating a man's property to his labor. Property, Locke said, is imbued with a man's labor and hence must be looked upon as an extension of his personality. As such, it presumably is entitled to the same protection as the owner's person. Locke displayed remarkable ingenuity in bringing all forms of property under the wing of his protecting philosophy—including land and inherited wealth. Yet it takes a strong self-interest in the conclusion to accept his argument more than half way. And the argument has always had greater appeal to the rising commercial interests, whose intellectual champion Locke has remained to this day, than to the receding feudal aristocracy with their absentee land holdings.

A more functional note is struck by the view that property must be protected if a man is to enjoy the fruits of his labor. We may be of different minds as to a man's moral right to these fruits—the internal revenue authorities plainly take a dim view of them. But it is in society's own interest to protect whatever a man does manage to accumulate, lest he stop accumulating altogether.

Again, it has been said that property is good and right insofar as it is actively used by its owner. The artisan working with his tools, even the factory owner managing his complex enterprise, score well under this doctrine. Out in the cold remain only the absentee coupon clippers and—logically—the widows and orphans living on a modest competence. Even R. H. Tawney, author of *The Acquisitive Society* and decidedly no friend of private property, saw some good in this sort of distinction.[1]

The historic defenses of property ring hollow in a good many spots. But the charges that have been flung against them likewise are more notable for lofty sentiment than for solid reasoning. Whether it be Proudhon's flat assertion that "property is theft," Veblen's sarcastic pronouncement that property started out as the proceeds of successful raids among primitive tribes and has retained its predatory character ever since, or Marx's ponderous demonstration that property arises from exploitation—these charges will convince chiefly those who already believe. They provide no compelling reason that property should be owned by "the people" instead of by the individual. Nor have the critics told us why, if private property is bad, the people of India should think it good and right that "the people" of France, the United States, or Russia should own and withhold from them the great wealth of their respective countries. Socialist thinking traditionally ends at home.

Certainly the last harsh word on the subject has not yet been said. But meanwhile the subject's evolution, as sometimes happens, has outdistanced the commentators. The complexion of property has changed.

To begin with, as I said before, property today is only one among several sources of income inequality. In years gone by, to be sure, to have a high income was almost synonymous with being a man of property. Agricultural land, urban real estate and commercial wealth were almost the only sources of a superior income. The growth of the managerial class, the professions and the bureaucracy (to the extent that one can call its pay "above average") has changed that. It has split the rich into the wealthy and the merely well paid. On a rough and ready calculation, less than half of total income inequality today has its roots in property income.

Secondly, property has become open-ended. As long as the bulk of property was represented by land, property was a closed corporation. X could acquire it only at the expense of Y, and bitterness over who should own a piece of the earth went deep. Today,

---

[1] R. H. Tawney, *The Acquisitive Society* (New York: Harcourt, Brace and Company, Harvest Books edition, 1946).

man-made property far exceeds that made by nature. Potential capital accumulation knows no ceiling, and my gain no longer has to be my neighbor's loss. A great broadening of property ownership bears witness to this development. On such terms, the demand for sharing or socializing the wealth loses much of its persuasiveness.

Nor have these remained the only changes in the nature of property. Once conceived of chiefly in terms of productive wealth, property today has branched out in the direction of consumers' property. Owner-occupied homes and durable consumer goods make up a goodly share of total wealth—homes alone account for $325 billion. And since more than half of our families are home owners, the have-nots, perhaps for the first time in history, have in this area become a minority.

Finally, property has changed by becoming less tangible and less absolute. A man's home may still be his castle, but the bulk of his wealth is likely to consist of rights and claims—to receive interest, to participate in profits, to share in the earning power of an enterprise. These ring less solid than real estate, and they are becoming increasingly tenuous, thanks to regulation, union pressure and the watchful eye of public opinion. Propertied men may still think of themselves as men of substance, but their property is becoming progressively less substantial.

Trends such as these—the diminished role of property in income distribution, the increasingly open-ended character of man-made wealth, the growth of consumer assets and the progressive sublimation of property—have taken much of the sting out of the argument. The defenders of property need no longer snatch at propositions that at times must have seemed an insult to the intelligence of their audience or a reflection on their own. The critics may take such oblique comfort as they can from the fact that in the United States they never stood a chance anyway. In the ensuing calm, both sides may proceed to re-examine private property on the basis, not of its rights and wrongs, but of its functional pros and cons.

The functional virtues of private property run parallel, in many respects, to those of private enterprise. The two, though not inseparable, always have maintained a close relationship. Hitler and Mussolini for a while succeeded in operating a system that combined private property with a minimum of private enterprise. That combination, however, seems to have been regarded as unstable even by its beneficiaries. The reverse system —private enterprise without private property—so far appears to have looked impractical even to the most arbitrary of dictators.

Private property, therefore, may be said to backstop the role of free enterprise. I had argued earlier that the chief virtue of a free economy is not its productivity but the support it gives to freedom. A dictatorial productivist economy may progress more rapidly in its own peculiar direction. But the impulse must come from compulsion. The chief virtue of a free economy, and implicitly of private property, is the protection it offers against the kind of government which would exert that kind of compulsion.

Private property accomplishes some further decentralization of its own. Power follows property, as has well been said. Property well distributed erects further defenses against concentrations of power, public or private. The caveat "well distributed" is a sizeable one, of course. In the past, property has often been more conspicuous for its concentration than for its dispersion. The public and the government then have both had to be on their guard against the "malefactors of great wealth." But even a small degree of dispersion protects against the kind of power concentration that would come from total government ownership of the means of production.

Private property lends another assist to private enterprise, by providing a powerful incentive. A high income may appear to be all the incentive there need be, for those who remember that "you can't take it with you." But the prestige, power, opportunity, security and further growth of income that come from property must not be underrated. And least of all should we overlook the incentive value of providing for one's family.

Here we come face to face with one of property's darker sides. Property earned has much in its favor. Property inherited is something very different. Yet to be meaningful, property must be capable of being passed on. In this new guise of inherited wealth it leaves many question marks. As an incentive, inherited property plainly works in reverse. William K. Vanderbilt may have gone a little far when he said that inherited wealth did to ambition what cocaine did to morality. But it probably does take an exceptional personality to resist the devitalizing effects of inheritance. And the rotation of society—from shirtsleeves to shirtsleeves—does not happen in three generations often enough to prevent inheritance from creating class distinctions and special privileges, and generally to keep certain people from thinking that they are worth money because they have it. The hereditary rich can argue with some plausibility that money does not make people happy. But the proposition would be more convincing if it were not employed quite so energetically to defend the continued possession of wealth.

The difficulties that hereditary property puts in the way of equality of opportunity we shall consider in more detail presently. For the time being it suffices to have drawn attention to one aspect of private property that is difficult to reconcile with some of our beliefs and values: its hereditary character.

Yet, the productive resources of the nation exist and must be administered somehow. The socialists once tried to persuade us that they knew a better way. Government ownership, they claimed, would do away with the difficulties posed by private ownership. In addition, it would provide new blessings of its own. Government ownership would remove inequalities of income; it would raise mass living standards by dividing up the incomes of the rich; it would humanize relations between management and labor; and it would inspire the worker with a new enthusiasm once he realized that he and not the boss was the true owner.

Such modest experience of socialized industry as Great Britain, France and other European countries have supplied does little to bear out these claims. Inequalities of income have not disappeared in socialized industries. The men who reach the upper echelons of these industries do not appear to be fundamentally different—unless they are political appointees—from those who advance under private ownership. Their liking for high salaries and perquisites is no less, their taste for equality no greater, than that of private managers.

Nor has the absence of dividends produced any large surplus available for higher wages. All that can be divided up among the workers without falling below the rate of capital formation prevailing under private ownership is the amount that the owners would have consumed. The sad capitalistic truth has been revealed that not only can't you take it with you—you can't even eat it all up down here. And it has been found not to matter greatly to the workers whether it is the capitalist or the state who is holding down wages in the interest of capital formation.

The more intimate bond between management and men likewise has proved something of a mirage. A large organization nationalized is still a large organization. Discipline and impersonality are as inevitable as before. If the government in power is a labor government, perhaps the management might be more accommodating on wage demands. But of this the workers can have no assurance; meanwhile, the potentialities of a strike suddenly take on a dimmer cast when it has to be directed against the government.

Hope for more enthusiastic performance of nationalized workers, finally, has proved most elusive of all. It is remarkable that this notion could take hold at all in Anglo-Saxon countries, where the idea of working for the government does not generally conjure up a vision of intense labor. The belief that men would work harder for the government would have seemed more appropriate to Karl Marx with his Prussian background. But honest idealists like Tawney made the idea of the dedicated worker an important part of their argumentation. When the British steel industry was about to be nationalized, enthusiastic laborites attributed a sudden upsurge in output to the anticipatory joy of the workers.

Subsequent experience seems to have been disillusioning. The essential point proved to be not who owned the plant, but who did not—in either case, the workers. "Mine is better than ours," said Benjamin Franklin. "Ours is better than theirs," has been the notion of socialists, but nationalization seems sadly to have failed to shake the workers' suspicion that the organization is, not "ours," but "theirs."

This short taste of socialism can hardly have been conclusive. Yet is has left its mark on socialist programs in many countries. Public control and equalization continue to hold the spotlight. Nationalization is fading into the background. The problem of private property, once a central concern, has lost its sting.

THE USE OF KNOWLEDGE
IN SOCIETY

—

By F. A. Hayek*

I

WHAT is the problem we wish to solve when we try to construct a rational economic order?

On certain familiar assumptions the answer is simple enough. *If* we possess all the relevant information, *if* we can start out from a given system of preferences and *if* we command complete knowledge of available means, the problem which remains is purely one of logic. That is, the answer to the question of what is the best use of the available means is implicit in our assumptions. The conditions which the solution of this optimum problem must satisfy have been fully worked out and can be stated best in mathematical form; put at their briefest, they are that the marginal rates of substitution between any two commodities or factors must be the same in all their different uses.

This, however, is emphatically *not* the economic problem which society faces. And the economic calculus which we have developed to solve this logical problem, though an important step toward the solution of the economic problem of society, does not yet provide an answer to it. The reason for this is that the "data" from which the economic calculus starts are never for the whole society "given" to a single mind which could work out the implications, and can never be so given.

The peculiar character of the problem of a rational economic order is determined precisely by the fact that the knowledge of the circumstances of which we must make use never exists in concentrated or integrated form, but solely as the dispersed bits

* The article below first appeared in the *American Economic Review,* September, 1945. It is reprinted by permission of the author.

of incomplete and frequently contradictory knowledge which all the separate individuals possess. The economic problem of society is thus not merely a problem of how to allocate "given" resources—if "given" is taken to mean given to a single mind which deliberately solves the problem set by these "data." It is rather a problem of how to secure the best use of resources known to any of the members of society, for ends whose relative importance only these individuals know. Or, to put it briefly, it is a problem of utilization of knowledge not given to anyone in its totality.

This character of the fundamental problem has, I am afraid, been obscured rather than illuminated by many of the recent refinements of economic theory, particularly by many of the uses made of mathematics. Though the problem with which I want primarily to deal in this paper is the problem of a rational economic oragnization, I shall in its course be led again and again to point to its close connections with certain methodological questions. Many of the points I wish to make are indeed conclusions toward which diverse paths of reasoning have unexpectedly converged. But as I now see these problems, this is no accident. It seems to me that many of the current disputes with regard to both economic theory and economic policy have their common origin in a misconception about the nature of the economic problem of society. This misconception in turn is due to an erroneous transfer to social phenomena of the habits of thought we have developed in dealing with the phenomena of Nature.

II

In ordinary language we describe by the word "planning" the complex of interrelated decisions about the allocation of our available resources. All economic activity is in this sense planning; and in any society in which many people collaborate, this planning, whoever does it, will in some measure have to be based on knowledge which, in the first instance, is not given to the planner but to somebody else, which somehow will have to be conveyed to the planner. The various ways in which the knowledge on which people base their plans is communicated to them is the crucial problem for any theory explaining the economic process. And the problem of what is the best way of utilizing knowledge initially dispersed among all the people is at least one of the main problems of economic policy—or of designing an efficient economic system.

The answer to this question is closely connected with that other question which arises here, that of *who* is to do the planning. It is about this question that all the dispute about "economic planning" centers. This is not a dispute about whether planning is to be done or not. It is a dispute as to whether planning is to be done centrally, by one authority for the whole economic system, or is to be divided among many individuals. Planning in the specific sense in which the term is used in contemporary controversy necessarily means central planning—direction of the whole economic system according to one unified plan. Competition, on the other hand, means decentralized planning by many separate persons. The halfway house between the two, about which many people talk but which few like when they see it, is the delegation of planning to organized industries, or, in other words, monopoly.

Which of these systems is likely to be more efficient depends mainly on the question under which of them we can expect that fuller use will be made of the existing knowledge. And this, in turn, depends on whether we are more likely to succeed in putting at the disposal of a single central authority all the knowledge which ought to be used but which is initially dispersed among many different individuals, or in conveying to the individuals such additional knowledge as they need in order to enable them to fit their plans in with those of others.

III

It will at once be evident that on this point the position will be different with respect to different kinds of knowledge; and the answer to our question will therefore largely turn on the relative importance of the different kinds of knowledge; those more likely to be at the disposal of particular individuals and those which we should with greater confidence expect to find in the possession of an authority made up of suitably chosen experts. If it is today so widely assumed that the latter will be in a better position, this is because one kind of knowledge, namely, scientific knowledge, now occupies so prominent a place in public imagination that we tend to forget that it is not the only kind that is relevant. It may be admitted that, so far as scientific knowledge is concerned, a body of suitably chosen experts may be in the best position to command all the best knowledge available—though this is, of course, merely shifting the difficulty to the problem of selecting the experts. What I wish to point out is that, even assuming that this problem can be readily solved, it is only a small part of the wider problem.

Today it is almost heresy to suggest that scientific knowledge is not the sum of all knowledge. But a little reflection will show that there is beyond question a body of very important but unorganized knowledge which cannot possibly be called scientific in the sense of knowledge of general rules: the knowledge of the particular circumstances of time and place. It is with respect to this that practically every individual has some advantage over all others, in that he possesses unique information of which beneficial use might be made, but of which use can be made only if the decisions depending on it are left to him or are made with his active cooperation. We need to remember only how much we have to learn in any occupation after we have completed our theoretical training, how big a part of our working life we spend learning particular jobs and how valuable an asset in all walks of life is knowledge of people, of local conditions and special circumstances. To know of and put to use a machine not fully employed, or somebody's skill which could be better utilized, or to be aware of a surplus stock which can be drawn upon during an interruption of supplies is socially quite as useful as the knowledge of better alternative techniques. And the shipper who earns his living from using otherwise empty or half-filled journeys of tramp steamers, or the estate agent whose whole knowledge is almost exclusively one of temporary opportunities, or the *arbitrageur* who gains from local differences of commodity prices are all performing eminently useful functions based on special knowledge of circumstances of the fleeting moment not known to others.

It is a curious fact that this sort of knowledge should today be generally regarded with a kind of contempt, and that anyone who by such knowledge gains an advantage over somebody better equipped with theoretical or technical knowledge is thought to have acted almost disreputably. To gain an advantage from better knowledge of facilities of communication or transport is sometimes regarded as almost dishonest, although it is quite as important that society make use of the best opportunities in this respect as in using the latest scientific discoveries. This prejudice has in a considerable measure affected the attitude toward commerce in general compared with that toward production. Even economists who regard themselves as definitely above the crude materialist fallacies of the past constantly commit the same mistake where activities directed toward the acquisition of such practical knowledge are concerned—apparently because in their scheme of things all such knowledge is supposed to be "given." The common idea now seems to be that all such knowledge should as a matter of course be readily at the command of everybody, and the reproach of irrationality leveled against the existing economic order is frequently based on the fact that it is not so available. This view disregards the fact that the method by which such knowledge can be made as widely available as possible is precisely the problem to which we have to find an answer.

IV

If it is fashionable today to minimize the importance of the knowledge of the particular circumstances of time and place, this is closely connected with the smaller importance which is now attached to change as such. Indeed, there are few points on which the assumptions made (usually only implicitly) by the "planners" differ from those of their opponents as much as with regard to the significance and frequency of changes which will make substantial alterations of production plans necessary. Of course, if detailed economic plans could be laid down for fairly long periods in advance and then closely adhered to, so that no further economic decisions of importance would be required, the task of drawing up a comprehensive plan governing all economic activity would appear much less formidable.

It is, perhaps, worth stressing that economic problems arise always and only in consequence of change. So long as things continue as before, or at least as they were expected to, there arise no new problems requiring a decision, no need to form a new plan. The belief that changes, or at least day-to-day adjustments, have become less important in modern times implies the contention that economic problems also have become less important. This belief in the decreasing importance of change is, for that reason, usually held by the same people who argue that the importance of economic considerations has been driven into the background by the growing importance of technological knowledge.

Is it true that, with the elaborate apparatus of modern production, economic decisions are required only at long intervals, as when a new factory is to be erected or a new process to be introduced? Is it true that, once a plant has been built, the rest is all more or less mechanical, determined by the character of the plant, and leaving little to be changed in adapting to the ever-changing circumstances of the moment?

The fairly widespread belief in the affirmative is not, so far as I can ascertain, borne out by the practical experience of the business man. In a competitive industry, at any rate—and such an industry alone can serve as a test—the task of keeping cost from rising requires constant struggle, absorbing a great part of the energy of the manager. How easy it is for an inefficient manager to dissipate the differentials on which profitability rests, and that it is possible, with the same technical facilities, to produce with a great variety of costs, are among the commonplaces of business experience which do not seem to be equally familiar in the study of the economist. The very strength of the desire, constantly voiced by producers and engineers, to be able to proceed untrammeled by considerations of money costs is eloquent testimony to the extent to which these factors enter into their daily work.

One reason economists are increasingly apt to forget about the constant small changes which make up the whole economic picture is probably their growing preoccupation with statistical aggregates, which show a very much greater stability than the movements of the detail. The comparative stability of the aggregates cannot, however, be accounted for—as the statisticians seem occasionally to be inclined to do—by the "law of large numbers" or the mutual compensation of random changes. The number of elements with which we have to deal is not large enough for such accidental forces to produce stability. The continuous flow of goods and services is maintained by constant deliberate adjustments, by new dispositions made every day in the light of circumstances not known the day before, by B stepping in at once when A fails to deliver. Even the large and highly mechanized plant keeps going largely because of an environment upon which it can draw for all sorts of unexpected needs: tiles for its roof, stationery for its forms and all the thousand and one kinds of equipment in which it cannot be self-contained and which the plans for the operation of the plant require to be readily available in the market.

This is, perhaps, also the point where I should briefly mention the fact that the sort of knowledge with which I have been concerned is knowledge of the kind which by its nature cannot enter into statistics and therefore cannot be conveyed to any central authority in statistical form. The statistics which such a central authority would have to use would have to be arrived at precisely by abstracting from minor differences between the things, by lumping together, as resources of one kind, items which differ as regards location, quality and other particulars, in a way which may be very significant for the specific decision. It follows from this that central planning based on statistical information by its nature cannot take direct account of these circumstances of time and place, and that the central planner will have to find some way or other in which the decisions depending on them can be left to the "man on the spot."

V

If we can agree that the economic problem of society is mainly one of rapid adaptation to changes in the particular circumstances of time and place, it would seem to follow that the ultimate decisions must be left to the people who are familiar with these circumstances, who know directly of the relevant changes and of the resources immediately available to meet them. We cannot expect that this problem will be solved by first communicating all this knowledge to a central board which, after integrating *all* knowledge, issues its orders. We must solve it by some form of decentralization. But this answers only part of our problem. We need decentralization because only thus can we insure that the knowledge of the particular circumstances of time and place will be promptly used. But the "man on the spot" cannot decide solely on the basis of his limited but intimate knowledge of the facts of his immediate surroundings. There still remains the problem of communicating to him such further information as he needs to fit his decisions into the whole pattern of changes of the large economic system.

How much knowledge does he need to do so successfully? Which of the events which happen beyond the horizon of his immediate knowledge are of relevance to his immediate decision, and how much of them need he know?

There is hardly anything that happens anywhere in the world that *might* not have an effect on the decision he ought to make. But he need not know of these events as such, nor of *all* their effects. It does not matter for him *why* at the particular moment more screws of one size than of another are wanted, *why* paper bags are more readily available than canvas bags or *why* skilled labor, or particular machine tools, have for the moment become more difficult to acquire. All that is significant for him is *how much more or less* difficult to procure they have become, compared with other things with which he is also concerned, or how much more or less urgently wanted are the alternative things he produces or uses. It is always a question of the relative importance of the particular things with which he is concerned, and the causes which alter their relative importance are of no interest to him beyond the effect on those concrete things of his own environment.

It is in this connection that what I have called the economic calculus proper helps us, at least by analogy, to see how this problem can be solved, and in fact is being solved, by the price system. Even the single controlling mind, in possession of all the data for some small, self-contained economic system, would not—every time some small adjustment in the allocation of resources had to be made—go explicitly through all the relations between ends and means which might possibly be affected. It is indeed the great contribution of the pure logic of choice that it has demonstrated conclusively that even such a single mind could solve this kind of problem only by constructing and constantly using rates of equivalence (or "values," or "marginal rates of substitution"), i.e., by attaching to each kind of scarce resource a numerical index which cannot be derived from any property possessed by that particular thing, but which reflects, or in which is condensed, its significance in view of the whole means-end structure. In any small change he will have to consider only these quantitative indexes (or "values") in which all the relevant information is concentrated; and by adjusting the quantities one by one, he can appropriately rearrange his dispositions without having to solve the whole puzzle *ab initio,* or without needing at any stage to survey it at once in all its ramifications.

Fundamentally, in a system where the knowledge of the relevant facts is dispersed among many people, prices can act to coordinate the separate actions of different people in the same way as subjective values help the individual to coordinate the parts of his plan. It is worth contemplating for a moment a very simple and commonplace instance of the action of the price system to see what precisely it accomplishees. Assume that somewhere in the world a new opportunity for the use of some raw material, say tin, has arisen, or that one of the sources of supply of tin has been eliminated. It does not matter for our purpose—and it is very significant that it does not matter—which of these two causes has made tin more scarce. All that the users of tin need to know is that some of the tin they used to consume is now more profitably employed elsewhere, and that in consequence they must economize tin. There is no need for the great majority of them even to know where the more urgent need has arisen, or in favor of what other needs they ought to husband the supply. If only some of them know directly of the new demand, and switch resources over to it, and if the people who are aware of the new gap thus created in turn fill it from still other sources, the effect will rapidly spread throughout the whole economic system and influence not only all the uses of tin, but also those of its substitutes and the substitutes of these substitutes, the supply of all the things made of tin, and their substitutes, and so on; and all this without the great majority

of those instrumental in bringing about these substitutions knowing anything at all about the original cause of these changes. The
whole acts as one market, not because any of its members survey
the whole field, but because their limited individual fields of
vision sufficiently overlap so that through many intermediaries
the relevant information is communicated to all. The mere fact
that there is one price for any commodity—or rather that local
prices are connected in a manner determined by the cost of
transport, etc.—brings about the solution which (it is just con-
ceptually possible) might have been arrived at by one single
mind possessing all the information which is, in fact, dispersed
among all the people involved in the process.

VI

We must look at the price system as such a mechanism for
communicating information if we want to understand its real
function—a function which, of course, fulfills less perfectly
as prices grow more rigid. (Even when quoted prices have become quite rigid, however, the forces which would operate
through changes in price still operate to a considerable extent
through changes in the other terms of the contract.) The most
significant fact about this system is the economy of knowledge
with which it operates, or how little the individual participants
need to know in order to be able to take the right action. In
abbreviated form, by a kind of symbol, only the most essential
information is passed on, and passed on only to those concerned.
It is more than a metaphor to describe the price system as a
kind of machinery for registering change, or a system of tele-
communications which enables individual producers to watch
merely the movement of a few pointers, as an engineer might
watch the hands of a few dials, in order to adjust their activities
to changes of which they may never know more than is reflected
in the price movement.

Of course, these adjustments are probably never "perfect" in
the sense in which the economist conceives of them in his
equilibrium analysis. But I fear that our theoretical habit of
approaching the problem with the assumption of more or less
perfect knowledge on the part of almost everyone has made us

somewhat blind to the true function of the price mechanism and led us to apply rather misleading standards in judging its efficiency. The marvel is that in a case like that of a scarcity of one raw material, without an order being issued, without more than perhaps a handful of people knowing the cause, tens of thousands of people whose identity could not be ascertained by months of investigation are made to use the material or its products more sparingly; i.e., they move in the right direction. This is enough of a marvel even if, in a constantly changing world, not all will hit it off so perfectly that their profit rates will always be maintained at the same constant or "normal" level.

I have deliberately used the word "marvel" to shock the reader out of the complacency with which we often take the working of this mechanism for granted. I am convinced that if it were the result of deliberate human design, and if the people guided by the price changes understood that their decisions have significance far beyond their immediate aim, this mechanism would have been acclaimed as one of the greatest triumphs of the human mind. Its misfortune is the double one that it is not the product of human design and that the people guided by it usually do not know why they are made to do what they do. But those who clamor for "conscious direction"—and who cannot believe that anything which evolved without design (and even without our understanding it) should solve problems which we should not be able to solve consciously—should remember this: the problem is precisely how to extend the span of our utilization of resources beyond the span of the control of any one mind and, therefore, how to dispense with the need of conscious control and how to provide inducements which will make the individuals do the desirable things without anyone having to tell them what to do.

The problem which we meet here is by no means peculiar to economics but arises in connection with nearly all truly social phenomena, with language and most of our cultural inheritance, and constitutes really the central theoretical problem of all social science. As Alfred Whitehead has said in another connection, "It is a profoundly erroneous truism, repeated by all copy-books and by eminent people when they are making speeches, that we should cultivate the habit of thinking what we are doing. The precise opposite is the case. Civilization advances by extending the number of important operations which we can perform without thinking about them." This is of profound significance in the social field. We make constant use of formulas, symbols and rules whose meaning we do not understand and through the use of which we avail ourselves of the assistance of knowledge which individually we do not possess. We have developed these practices and institutions by building upon habits and institutions which have proved successful in their own sphere and which have in turn become the foundation of the civilization we have built up.

The price system is just one of those formations which man has learned to use (though he is still very far from having learned to make the best of it) after he had stumbled upon it without understanding it. Through it not only a division of labor but also a coordinated utilization of resources based on an equally divided knowledge has become possible. The people who like to deride any suggestion that this may be so usually distort the argument by insinuating that it asserts that by some miracle just that sort of system has spontaneously grown up which is best suited to modern civilization. It is the other way round: Man has been able to develop that division of labor on which our civilization is based because he happened to stumble upon a method which made it possible. Had he not done so he might still have developed some other, altogether different, type of civilization, something like the "state" of the termite ants, or some other altogether unimaginable type. All that we can say is that nobody has yet succeeded in designing an alternative system in which certain features of the existing one can be preserved which are dear even to those who must violently assail it—such as, particularly, the extent to which the individual can choose his pursuits and consequently freely use his own knowledge and skill.

VII

It is in many ways fortunate that the dispute about the indispensability of the price system for any rational calculation in a complex society is now no longer conducted entirely between camps holding different political views. The thesis that without the price system we could not preserve a society based on such extensive division of labor as ours was greeted with a howl of derision when it was first advanced by von Mises twenty-five years ago. Today the difficulties which some still find in accepting it are no longer mainly political, and this makes for an atmosphere much more conducive to reasonable discussion. When we find Leon Trotsky arguing that "economic accounting is unthinkable without market relations"; when Professor Oscar Lange promises Professor von Mises a statue in the marble halls of the future Central Planning Board; and when Professor Abba P. Lerner rediscovers Adam Smith and emphasizes that the essential utility of the price system consists in inducing the individual, while seeking his own interest, to do what is in the general interest, the differences can indeed no longer be ascribed to political prejudice. The remaining dissent seems clearly to be due to purely intellectual, and, more particularly, methodological differences.

A recent statement by Professor Joseph Schumpeter in his *Capitalism, Socialism, and Democracy* provides a clear illustration of one of the methodological differences which I have in mind. Its author is preeminent among those economists who approach economic phenomena in the light of a certain branch of positivism. To him these phenomena accordingly appear as objectively given quantities of commodities impinging directly upon each other, almost, it would seem, without any intervention of human minds. Only against this background can I account for the following (to me startling) pronouncement. Professor Schumpeter argues that the possibility of a rational calculation in the absence of markets for the factors of production follows for the theorist "from the elementary proposition that consumers in evaluating ('demanding') consumers' goods *ipso facto* also evaluate the means of production which enter into the production of these goods." [1]

---

[1] J. Schumpeter, *Capitalism, Socialism, and Democracy* (New York: Harper & Bros., 1942), p. 175. Professor Schumpeter is, I believe, also the original author of the myth that Pareto and Barone have "solved" the problem of socialist calculation. What they, and many others, did was merely to state the conditions which a rational allocation of resources would have to satisfy, and to point out that these were essentially the same as the con-

Taken literally, this statement is simply untrue. The consumers do nothing of the kind. What Professor Schumpeter's *ipso facto* presumably means is that the valuation of the factors of production is implied in, or follows necessarily from, the valuation of consumers' goods. But this, too, is not correct. Implication is a logical relationship which can be meaningfully asserted only of propositions simultaneously present to one and the same mind. It is evident, however, that the values of the factors of production do not depend solely on the valuation of the consumers' good but also on the conditions of supply of the various factors of production. Only to a mind to which all these facts were simultaneously known would the answer necessarily follow from the facts given to it. The practical problem, however, arises precisely because these facts are never so given to a single mind, and because, in consequence, it is necessary that in the solution of the problem knowledge should be used that is dispersed among many people.

The problem is thus in no way solved if we can show that all the facts, *if* they were known to a single mind (as we hypothetically assume them to be given to the observing economist), would uniquely determine the solution; instead, we must show how a solution is produced by the interactions of people each of whom possesses only partial knowledge. To assume all the knowledge to be given to a single mind in the same manner in which we assume it to be given to us as the explaining economists is to assume the problem away and to disregard everything that is important and significant in the real world.

That an economist of Professor Schumpeter's standing should thus have fallen into a trap which the ambiguity of the term "datum" sets to the unwary can hardly be explained as a simple error. It suggests rather that there is something fundamentally wrong with an approach which habitually disregards an essential

---

ditions of equilibrium of a competitive market. This is something altogether different from showing how the allocation of resources satisfying these conditions can be found in practice. Pareto himself (from whom Barone has take practically everything he has to say), far from claiming to have solved the practical problem, in fact explicitly denies that it can be solved without the help of the market. See his *Manuel d'économie pure* (2d ed., 1927), pp. 233–34. The relevant passage is quoted in an English translation at the beginning of my article on "Socialist Calculation: The Competitive 'Solution,'" in *Economica*, N. S. VIII, No. 26 (May, 1940), 125.

part of the phenomena with which we have to deal: the unavoidable imperfection of man's knowledge and the consequent need for a process by which knowledge is constantly communicated and acquired. Any approach, such as that of much of mathematical economics with its simultaneous equations, which in effect starts from the assumption that people's *knowledge* corresponds with the objective *facts* of the situation, systematically leaves out what it is our main task to explain. I am far from denying that in our system equilibrium analysis has a useful function to perform. But when it comes to the point where it misleads some of our leading thinkers into believing that the situation which it describes has direct relevance to the solution of practical problems, it is time that we remember that it does not deal with the social process at all and that it is no more than a useful preliminary to the study of the main problem.

HOW A PRIVATE–ENTERPRISE SYSTEM SOLVES THE BASIC ECONOMIC PROBLEMS

—

By George Leland Bach*

How the Price System Decides What to Produce

Under a private-enterprise, free-price system, consumers control what is produced. Prices register consumer preferences through the amount of money consumers spend on various goods and services. The more you want something, the more money you will spend on it and the higher price you will be willing to pay for it. How much people want beefsteak, autos, and movie queens is measured by how much they spend on each; and it is on this basis that the price system decides which are the most important goods and services to be produced.

But in order to count, consumers' demands have to be backed up with dollars. No matter how badly a poor family may want a Buick and a fine house, its desires become effective in the market only to the extent they are backed up by the ability to pay for such things. The price mechanism is hardboiled, impersonal. It produces Cadillacs for millionaires when poor youngsters have no toys. Prices reflect not how much consumers "need" goods and services, but how much they are willing and able to pay for them.

* George Leland Bach, economist, holds an LL.D. from Grinnell College (1956) and a Ph.D. from the University of Chicago (1940). He became professor and head of the department of economics at the Carnegie Institute of Technology in 1946 and dean of the Graduate School of Industrial Administration there in 1949. He is a member of the American Finance Association and the American Economic Association (executive committee 1959–60), and chairman of the National Task Force on Economic Education. In 1963 he was named Ford research professor at Stanford University.

Bach has written *Inflation: A Study in Economics, Ethics, and Politics* (1958) and *Management and Corporation* (1960) among other books, and numerous articles for professional journals.

The article below is from *Economics* (4th ed., 1963) a textbook by Bach, and is reprinted here by permission of the author and Prentice-Hall, Inc.

How the Price System Gets the Goods Produced

Businessmen are out to make profits. Profits are found where selling prices are higher than costs. Thus businessmen will move to those industries where consumers bid prices up, and where their own ingenuity and other factors can bring costs down. Workers and owners of other productive resources will move toward higher pay and away from lower-pay opportunities, insofar as it's pay they're after; if it's not pay, the system adjusts to their preference for work in lower-pay but otherwise more attractive industries. This combination of consumer demand, workers' job preferences and the businessman's desire for profits gets the goods produced that consumers want most, at the lowest possible cost.

Thus the businessman is essentially a link between consumers and productive resources. His social function is to organize productive activity in the most efficient (lowest-cost) way possible, and to channel productive resources toward the industries where consumer demand is strongest. Profits are the mainspring of the system—the carrot in front of the profit-seeker. In seeking profits, the businessman (perhaps quite involuntarily) performs a vital social function.

How the Price System Distributes Products

Who gets the goods that are produced? The price system gives them to those who have the desire and the income to buy them. There are two steps in this process of distribution.

The first is the distribution of money income. We earn our incomes primarily by working for businessmen, helping to produce the goods and services consumers want. The prices we get for our services depend on how much we are worth to the businesses we work for. Very roughly, competition forces the businessman to pay each of us about what we contribute to the sale value of what he is producing. The incomes we receive in this way largely determine what we can afford to buy.

The second step is the distribution of goods and services among those with money income to pay for them. The price of each commodity is bid up until the buyers least able or willing to pay for it are eliminated. This does not necessarily mean that low-income buyers are eliminated completely. Often it means that they can afford only a few units at the price established, while the higher-income groups can afford more. Poor people buy steaks, but not many. In other cases, such as mink coats and fine houses, the poor are eliminated.

How the Price System Decides Between Present and Future: Economic Growth

Productive resources may be used to produce either for current consumption or for capital accumulation (that is, machinery, buildings and so on, which will help increase future production). Here again the private-enterprise system depends largely on the free choices of consumers and the decisions of profit-seekers, intergrated through the investment and money markets, to make this choice.

Each person decides how much of his income he wants to save. Each business does the same. If the sum of all such savings is large, profit-seekers will find it easier to borrow funds, and they will be led to invest in building new machinery and other long-term productive equipment for future production. At the same time, the switch of consumers' incomes from current consumption to savings makes the profit opportunities in producing goods for current consumption relatively less attractive. Businessmen will gain by producing machinery, buildings and factory equipment rather than shoes, food and tennis rackets. The pattern of production will be shifted toward capital accumulation until production of consumers' and producers' goods corresponds to the division of current incomes between consumption and saving. Economic growth speeds up. Here is a mechanism by which the price system regulates the rate of economic growth.

Solving All the Problems Simultaneously

These four major decisions are not made separately. Rather, they are all completely interdependent. The economic system is a huge, interconnected set of markets, each with many buyers and sellers. The end result is the outcome of millions of free, individual decisions, by people largely concerned with their own private welfare. Since most buyers buy in many different markets, what they buy of one good affects what they will buy of another.

Most sellers must compete with many other sellers for the labor they hire, the raw materials they use, the dollars they borrow to build their plants. The process of production both produces goods to meet consumer demands and generates incomes for workers who are in turn consumers. Each consumer constantly chooses between buying something now with his income, or saving. All these things go on simultaneously.

COMPETITION

—

By William J. Baumol and Lester V. Chandler*

BY competition we mean, of course, rivalry among buyers and sellers. It includes rivalry of seller against seller, or buyer against buyer and of buyer against seller. Moreover, we usually assume that the primary motive of each buyer and seller is to promote his own advantage.

Some critics of free-enterprise systems have alleged that these are not systems at all but only anarchies—that they have no logic, and that they afford no means of welding productive factors into a coordinated economic process to satisfy human wants. It is easy to show that this crude argument is fallacious. Whether or not competition is a better control system that any other, the fact is that it does work; systems relying largely on competitive control have achieved high and rising levels of productivity, and they have somehow determined the composition of output, the relative prices of the various types of output, the allocation of resources and the distribution of income among the members of the community.

---

* William J. Baumol, educator, received his Ph.D. from London University in 1949 and in 1954 became a professor at Princeton University. He was a consultant for Mathematica, Inc., at Princeton; a member of the executive committee of the American Economic Association; a Guggenheim fellow in 1957–58; he is a fellow of the Econometric Society.

His writings include *Business Behavior, Value, and Growth* (1959) and *Economic Theory and Operations Analysis* (1960, with L. V. Chandler).

Lester V. Chandler, economist, received his Ph.D. at Yale University in 1934. He became Gordon S. Rentschler professor of economics at Princeton in 1950, and in 1955 was made chairman of Princeton's Department of Economics and Sociology. He is a member of the American Economic Association and the American Finance Association. *Preface to Economics* (1947) and *Inflation in the United States* (1951) are among his works.

"Competition" is excerpted from *Economic Processes and Policies* (1954). It is reprinted by permission of Harper & Row, Inc.

In brief outline, this is the logic of the competitive systems: (1) The goals of production—the particular types and amounts of goods and services to be produced—are set by the free choices of consumers. This is often called consumers' sovereignty. Consumers have at their disposal certain amounts of money income which they are free to spend as they see fit for the various types of output that might be produced by business firms. They communicate their choices to the market and bring pressure on business firms to adjust output to these choices by the way they spend their money incomes. In effect, they cast "dollar ballots" for the different types of output.

(2) Production and trade are carried on by many business firms, each intent on making as much net money income as it can. But these firms can make maximum profits only if they use the available productive factors to turn out the particular types and amounts of goods and services that consumers demand. If they produce things for which consumers cast no dollar ballots they will obviously be unable to sell them. If "too much" of some article is produced relative to consumers' demands, its price will fall so low as to penalize its producers. If "too little" of some article is produced relative to consumers' demands, its price will be so high as to encourage an increase in its production. Thus business firms can realize their desire to avoid losses and maximize profits only by adjusting output to consumers' choices as expressed in their market demands.

These ideas are beautifully expressed in Adam Smith's *Wealth of Nations,* the work which was to serve as a chief source of inspiration to those who favored a free-enterprise system.

In almost every other race of animals each individual, when it is grown up to maturity, is entirely independent, and in its natural state has occasion for the assistance of no other living creature. But man has almost constant occasion for the help of his brethren, and it is in vain for him to expect it from their benevolence only. He will be more likely to prevail if he can interest their self-love in his favour and shew them that it is for their own advantage to do for him what he requires of them. Whoever offers to another a bargain of any kind, proposes to do this. Give me that which I want, and you shall have this which you want, is the meaning of every such offer; and it is in this manner that we obtain from one another the far greater part of those good offices which we stand in need of. It is not from the benevolence of the butcher, the brewer, or the baker, that we expect our dinner, but from their regard to their own interest. We address ourselves, not to their humanity but to their self-love, and never talk to them of our own necessities but of their advantages. Nobody but a begger chuses to depend chiefly upon the benevolence of his fellow-citizens.[1]

As every individual, therefore, endeavours as much as he can both to employ his capital in the support of domestic industry, and so to direct that industry that its produce may be of the greatest value; every individual necessarily labours to render the annual revenue of the society as great as he can. He generally, indeed, neither intends to promote the public interest, nor knows how much he is promoting it. By preferring the support of domestic to that of foreign industry, he intends only his own security; and by directing that industry in such a manner as its produce may be of the greatest value, he intends only his own gain, and he is in this, as in many other cases, led by an invisible hand to promote an end which was no part of his intention. Nor is it always the worse for the society that it was no part of it. By pursuing his own interest he frequently promotes that of the society more effectually than when he really intends to promote it. I have never known much good done by those who affected to trade for the public good. It is an affectation, indeed, not very common among merchants, and very few words need be employed in dissuading them from it.[2]

To show that the argument is not mystical in spite of the reference to "the invisible hand" we shall describe competitive process in more detail. As a first step we shall identify the various participants.

PARTICIPANTS IN THE COMPETITIVE PROCESS

Ignoring the government for the moment, we can divide the participants in the competitive process into three broad classes: (1) households, which receive and dispose of money incomes; (2) business firms, which produce and trade goods and services; and (3) the owners of productive factors, who either use their

[1] *Wealth of Nations*, Book I, chap. ii.
[2] *Ibid.*, Book IV, chap. ii.

own factors or sell their services to business firms or in some cases directly to households. It is immediately evident that each individual is likely to be a member of two or more of these groups. Thus a worker may be both a seller of his labor services and the head of a household. Or a man may be both the head of a business firm and the head of a household. Our functional classification is useful, however, for it enables us to analyze the various motivations and functions of each person or institution in the competitive process.

A. *Households*

By households we mean families and certain other small groups that pool their money incomes and as a unit determine how these will be disposed of. We shall concentrate on this income receipt and disposal function of households. We deal with the household rather than a person as the basic consuming unit to avoid becoming ensnarled in the difficult question, "Who determines a family's spending pattern?" It is true, of course, that some production occurs within the household; dishwashing, cooking, housecleaning and other similar examples come quickly to mind. But this part of production does not enter into the competitive market process and we shall ignore it.

Each household receives some amount of money income. Most of it is usually received as compensation for the services of productive factors owned by the household—wages and salaries for labor, interest on savings, rent on real estate and profits for the services of being a business owner. Each family has a wide degree of freedom in disposing of its money income, and it is to be presumed that each will spend the money in the way that appears to be most advantageous to it. Some of this income may be saved; this part we shall consider later. The part spent for consumption will be spread among the many available types of goods and services in accordance with the family's tastes. In making such choices, each family in effect casts dollar ballots for the various types of output.

But the amount of any good or service that a household will buy depends not only on its income and tastes but also on the price of that particular good or service relative to the prices of other things. For example, the cheaper beef is, relative to other things, the more of it the family is likely to purchase. A statement giving the different amounts of beef which the family will buy at each different beef price is called that family's *demand schedule* for beef.

Owing to the differences in tastes as well as to the differences in incomes, different households are likely to have quite different demand schedules for each of the various types of goods and services. One household may be willing to buy a large amount of article A at a high price, whereas another will buy none of it at that price.

By adding together the many individual household demand schedules for each product we can get the *total market demand schedule* for that product. Thus, the total market demand for article A at a price of $10 is the sum of the amounts that all households would buy at that price. And the total market demand at a price of $5 is the sum of the amounts that all households would buy at that price. The same is true at all other levels of prices.

Thus we find that with any given total amount of money income for households, any given distribution of this money income among the households and any given set of tastes of the households, there will be in the market at any time a complex of demand relationships. For any particular good or service this will take the form of a market demand schedule which usually has this characteristic: the larger the amount of the article offered for sale, the lower will be the price at which all of it will be purchased; and the smaller the amount of the article offered for sale, the higher will be the price at which all of it can find purchasers.

These total market demand schedules for each of the various possible types of output, reflecting consumers' choices, are the guides to production. Or, as it is sometimes said, they are the means by which consumers exercise sovereignty over the market. If producers wish to make maximum profits they must adjust their activities to consumers' choices as indicated by the series of market demand schedules for the various possible types of output. This brings us to the role of business firms in the competitive process.

B. *Business Firms*

Production and trade are carried on by millions of business firms. The primary purpose of each firm is to make net money income in the form of profits. Enterprisers create new firms, discontinue old firms, expand and contract the size of their firms, vary rates of output in their plants and shift their production from one type of output to another as opportunities for greater profits or smaller losses appear.

These millions of firms compete with each other in two principal ways. (1) They compete for the buyer's dollars. We are all familiar with the fact that the producers of the same type of output, such as radios, compete for the consumers' dollars. But in a broader sense every producer competes with every other producer for consumers' dollars. Thus the sellers of radios, autos, cigarettes, movie admissions and all other goods and services compete for the buyer's dollar votes. (2) They compete for production factors. All firms enter the market and compete for labor, for the use of natural resources, for the rental of buildings and other durable equipment and for the use of money savings. Each firm will vary its purchases of each type of productive factor according to their respective prices. That is, each firm has a demand schedule for the services of each type of productive factor.

It is important to note that a firm's demand for each type of productive factor is a *derived demand*—a demand derived from the market demand for the firm's output. The firm buys the services of productive factors only because they are capable of producing goods or services that can be sold in the market for money. And both the amount of any productive factor that a firm will buy and the price it will be willing to pay for the factor depend on how much successive units of the factor can be expected to add to the value of the firm's output.

C. *The Owners of Productive Factors*

The owners of the various types of productive factors make up the third group of participants in the competitive process. These include workers of all kinds who are the sellers of their own services, owners of natural resources who offer them for use, owners of buildings and other durable capital goods who offer them for rent, and owners of money savings who offer them for loan or shares of ownership. Subject to some qualification, these owners wish to get as much money income as they can and will therefore sell the use of their productive factors to the firms that offer the highest price. Whenever it is profitable to do so, they will shift their factors not only from firm to firm within a given industry but also among firms in different industries.

D. *Summary*

In short, there are three broad classes of participants in the competitive process. Households provide the ultimate guides to production through their demand schedules in the market. Business firms, intent on making as much profit as they can, organize and direct production and hire productive factors. And the owners of productive factors sell them to the firms that will bid the most for them. We can now proceed to see how competition among all these participants controls economic processes.

COMPETITIVE EQUILIBRIUM:
GENERAL CHARACTERISTICS

A. *Adjustment to Constant Demand Schedules*

Let us look first at the process by which competition adjusts output, prices and the allocation of resources to a set of household demand schedules that remain constant during the adjustment period. We assume that consumers' choices, as reflected in their market demand schedules, remain fixed, but that the demand for each product is such that the more of it that is offered, the lower will be its price, and the less of it that is offered, the higher will be its price.

We may expect that the price of any commodity will rise if the demand for it exceeds the supply and that it will fall if more is offered for sale than consumers are willing to buy. Only if demand and supply are equal will there be no tendency for the price to change. Only then can we have competitive equilibrium.

Business firms, intent on avoiding losses and making as much profit as possible, adjust their supply to consumer demand schedules. They will avoid producing any item whose prices are so low as to cause losses or to yield profits below those in other lines. The increased scarcity then tends to raise the prices of these items. At the same time, they will increase their output of items whose prices are so high as to yield larger profits than could be secured elsewhere. This tends to lower the prices of these items. Thus the process of adjustment will continue, with producers decreasing their output of items that yield only losses or lower profits than can be made in other lines, and increasing their output of any items on which profits are higher than in other lines. The adjustment process will end only when the relative prices of the various types of output, the rates of output and the allocation of factors are such that no one finds it profitable to make any further adjustment. This is what we mean by competitive equilibrium.

Three important characteristics of competitive equilibrium should be noted. (1) Prices are such as to clear the market. That is, all the supply that is offered at these prices finds buyers and (at these prices) there is no unsatisfied demand. (2) Prices are such that firms in the aggregate have no net incentive to make further changes in either the types or the rates of their output. (3) The allocation and prices of productive factors are such that the owners of these factors have no incentive to make any further net shifts from one industry to another. If all these conditions are not met competitive equilibrium has not been established.

B. *Adjustment to Changes in Consumers' Demands*

In the preceding section we outlined the process of adjusting prices, the composition of output and the allocation of resources to a set of constant consumer demand schedules. Let us now consider the process of adjusting to changes in consumers' preferences. Suppose that consumers decrease their demands for radios and increase their demands for television sets. In the radio industry the first effect will be to lower the prices of radios, or at least to decrease the number that can be sold at the old prices. Under these new conditions, radio production will be less profitable than before and at least some of the producers will probably suffer losses. Some may even go bankrupt. In any case, the rate of radio output will decline and smaller amounts of productive factors will be used in radio production. This reduction of output will continue until the amount of output remaining can be sold at prices high enough to yield profits as high as those in other lines.

The rise of consumers' demands for television sets will raise their prices, or at least increase the number of sets that can be sold at the old prices. This greater profitability will increase the output of television sets and cause more productive factors to be employed for this purpose. Some new firms may set up business in the television industry. This expansion will continue until television output has been increased so much and prices have receded to such an extent that profits in the industry will be no higher than those elsewhere.

We see that resources will have been reallocated from radio to television production in accord with changed consumers' desires. This is but one example of the general process of adjusting output and the allocation of resources to consumers' preferences as indicated by their market demand schedules.

C. *Competitive Sanctions*

We noted earlier that a control system can succeed only if it employs powerful sanctions. The competitive system meets this test. It uses both rewards and penalties to induce business firms to adjust to consumers' demands. Those that adjust the types and rates of their output to consumers' demands promptly, especially those that correctly anticipate changes in consumers' demands, may reap large profits. But those that persist in producing things that consumers do not want or that contribute to the overproduction of a particular type of product are penalized by losses. If they get too far out of line with consumers' demands they will be eliminated from the market by bankruptcy.

The same is true of labor and other productive factors. Those that are shifted promptly to the production of things that consumers want most may be rewarded by steady employment and high incomes. But those who persist in offering their services for the production of things that consumers do not want at all or will buy only at very low prices are likely to be penalized by low incomes or unemployment.

D. *Competitive Promotion of Efficiency*

Competition brings powerful pressures on business firms to improve their efficiency—that is, to get as large a value of output as they can from the value of inputs they use up in the process of production. For this purpose it uses both rewards and penalties. A firm can reap large profits by pioneering in reducing its costs below those of its competitors. Thus every firm has a strong incentive to develop and employ technological innovations, to achieve optimum size, to use the most economical combination of productive resources and to do anything else that will reduce its costs relative to its selling prices. The hope or reward for pioneering is supplanted by an even more powerful sanction—the fear of penalty for being a laggard. The firms that fail to lower costs as much as their competitors may suffer losses and even bankruptcy as their more efficient competitors lower the selling prices of their products, or bid up the prices of productive factors, or both.

The principal results of this competitive race to raise efficiency and lower costs may be to lower prices to consumers, or to increase the incomes paid to productive factors, or both. But any firm that lags behind in this race may be eliminated by losses or even by bankruptcy. It is therefore easy to understand why competition has been such a powerful force for continuous technological change and rising efficiency. This includes not only the development and use of cheaper methods of production but also the development of new products that will meet the approval of consumers.

COMPETITION AND THE SOLUTION OF THE BASIC ECONOMIC PROBLEMS

Though it has already been implied in our discussion, we should note specifically that the competitive process provides a simultaneous solution of the basic economic problems mentioned earlier—the determination of the overall rate of output, the composition and pricing of output, the allocation of resources and the distribution of income.

The Overall Rate of Output

. . . The overall rate of output of business firms is determined by the competitive interactions of buyers' demands, the responses of business firms and the supplies of productive factors. Buyers' payments provide the rewards for production, and to these demands of buyers business firms adjust both the overall rate of output and the total amount of productive factors employed.

The Composition and Pricing of Output

As we have already seen, the types of goods and services to be produced, the amounts of each and the relative prices of the various types are determined by buyers' demands and the supplies offered by business firms as they try to make as much profit as possible.

The Allocation of Productive Factors

This same competitive process also allocates the scarce supply of productive factors among their many alternative uses. As we have already seen, each of the millions of business firms has a derived demand for the various types of natural resources, labor and capital—a demand based on the amount that the productive factor can add to the value of the firm's output. At the same time, the owners of the productive factors stand ready to supply them to the firms that will offer the most for them. These demand and supply conditions determine a market price for the use of each type of productive factor—a wage or salary rate for each type of labor, a rental rate for each type of natural resource and an interest rate on capital.

These prices of the productive factors serve as an allocative or rationing device. Each firm will presumably hire additional units of productive factors so long as these additional units will add to the value of its output and amount greater than the price that must be paid for the factor. For example, if the price of a particular type of labor is $10 a day, each firm will hire as many man-days of that labor as will add more than $10 to the value of its output. But we may assume that no firm will hire at $10 any man-days of this labor that will add less than this amount to the value of its output. Thus the price of the factor, which is determined by competition, rations the available supply. It allocates the factors to those who can make them add the most to the value of output and denies these factors to those who cannot derive so much value from their use.

The Distribution of Income

The competitive process which we have just described also determines the distribution of income among the owners of the various types of productive factors. As we saw above, it determines the wage or salary rates for the various types of labor, rental rates for the various types of natural resources, interest rates on capital and profits of enterprisers. The income of any family depends on the prices of the productive factors it offers for use and on the amounts of these factors it has.

We have seen that economic control in the United States and other similar economies rests primarily in two entities, the government and market competition. The essence of the free-enterprise system is the fact that by far the larger part of the control function devolves on the market. We may again note three things which the market tends to accomplish. (1) It makes for the efficient operation of the firm. (2) It promotes responsiveness of output composition to consumers' desires. (3) It organizes the productive system and arranges for the factors of production to be where they are needed when they are needed.

The market is thus, at least in its ideal form, an amazingly efficient means of giving effect to the desires of the members of an economy, insofar as this is permitted by the scarcity of resources. Is it not surprising that, practically without central supervision and without any centrally formulated and administered overall plan, consumers find their desires catered to—provided they have the money to pay—and that the great complex of processes competing for raw materials and productive factors is so organized that the goods the consumer wants are there when he asks for them?

THE VALUES OF COMPETITION

—

By Clare E. Griffin*

THE values of competition . . . relate to our effectiveness as producers and also to the other elements of opportunity and freedom which are essential to our concept of a good society. These values can be best summarized by recalling the central feature of competition. It is the rivalry between people of one economic class to gain the patronage of those in another class or group. Among people who are free to direct their patronage as they wish, that rivalry must consist of efforts to offer a *quid pro quo* which will be attractive to the members of the opposite group—buyers or sellers.

This general statement suggests that the value of a competitive system consists in the pervasive and continuing efforts on the part of people generally, both buyers and sellers, to conduct their affairs in such ways as will be agreeable to those with whom they are dealing. More specifically, certain values of competition can be enumerated. First, a competitive system assumes and provides a great many centers of decision; each person must feel free under such a system to make his appeals to others on bases that seem best to him. Such a situation, therefore, makes for variety and presents the opportunity for testing the effectiveness and the values of different methods of production, sales techniques and other elements of economic activity in the marketplace. It is believed that this principle of decentrali-

---

* Clare E. Griffin received his Ph.D. from the University of Illinois in 1918, and was dean of the School of Business Administration and director of the Bureau of Business Research at the University of Michigan from 1927 to 1943. In 1943 he was named Fred M. Taylor professor of business economics and from 1943 to 1946 was on the research staff of the Committee for Economic Development. He has served as an economic consultant to various organizations and holds memberships in the American Economic Association and the American Marketing Association.

Two of his works are *Enterprise in a Free Society* (1949) and *An Economic Approach to Anti-Trust Problems* (1951).

"The Values of Competition" is taken from the former book, published by Richard D. Irwin, Inc., and is reprinted by permission of the author.

zation or decision making makes better use of the potentialities of an intelligent and imaginative people than could any system of centralized authority.

A special reason for assigning this value to diversity is our interest in economic progress. The ideas of new and improved methods of production or of new products to be offered do not occur to all members of the society at once; nor would all members of the society or even their common representatives in a planned economy be willing to adopt new methods or to offer new products. Under a system of decentralization, it is not essential that common agreement should exist. It is only necessary that a small minority should be genuinely progressive; the rivalry of the others and their desire to preserve their position will force them to follow the more progressive leaders, even though if left to themselves they might prefer to continue in their old ways. Thus, the creative minority does exercise great influence over the majority. This is the basic reason that too much self-government of business or other devices by which the majority in any line of activity can impose their will upon the minority are dangerous to progress, in spite of supposed values which such devices have for stability. Examples of the influence of such an aggressive minority in a competitive society are numerous. For instance, the automobile industry came into existence and has advanced not by any general agreement of producers or of the whole society that this method of transportation had merit; rather, a few innovators who did not have to secure the approval of any responsible group could set a pace which the others had to emulate in order to stay in the race. On this ground we expect a noncompetitive society—either one dominated by private monopolies or one controlled by a monopolistic state—to lack the progressive qualities of a competitive society. Particularly, according to this view, a state-controlled system is likely to be a conservative one—perhaps even more conservative than a system of private industrial monopolies, for such "monopolies" would at least face interindustry competition.

Second, under a system of competition, the most feasible way for a seller to advance his own interests is by producing more and better goods and services. It is true that in many situations the returns to sellers could be increased by creating scarcities as well as by striving for abundance. While the deliberate restriction of production and thus the enchancement of the value of the seller's product may be attractive to the sellers of that product, it is clear that, from the point of view of the society as a whole, such a program spells economic suicide; it is as true today as in the time of Adam Smith that the annual income of a country depends upon its annual production. The merit of competition in this respect is that it is unprofitable for an individual competitor to follow such a device. A competitive system, therefore, establishes a parallelism between the individual interests of sellers and the larger requirements of the society.

Third, the rivalry of sellers for the patronage of buyers and the rivalry of buyers for the patronage of sellers, although it does constitute strife in a certain sense, tends to remove conflict between the members of the different economic groups. Thus, rivalry eliminates or moderates the strife that would exist between such power groups as the mass of sellers and an organization of buyers. It is highly desirable that such clashes of power groups should be avoided because they breed disunity; and, moreover, a clash of interests between such functional groups does not provide any automatic way for the solution of differences. It may lead instead to an impasse in which production and economic activity may come to a stop. An example of such an impasse is presented in protracted strikes.

Fourth, a closely related value of competition is that it has the effect of limiting power. Under this system the power of any one seller, for example, to determine the conditions upon which the buyers will obtain his product is limited by the efforts of other sellers to gain the patronage of the same buyers. Likewise, the buyer—either the buyer of goods or the employer of services—will be unable to impose terms of purchase or payment which would be most agreeable to him because there are competing buyers or employers whose bids must be taken into account. Indeed, one of the ways of stating the essential feature of competition is that under competition every person must consider not only his own desires but the rival offers of others in his own economic group. Thus, the power of any one individual or group is limited by that of others: it provides the protection of checks and balances.

Fifth, at the same time that it reduces power, the principle of competition increases the freedom of individuals. It does this in two ways. On the one side, as suggested above, it increases the freedom of individual enterprisers to make offers that to them seem best; and, on the other side, it increases the freedom of the persons to whom these offers are made. This latter aspect needs particularly to be stressed because, in practice, freedom consists of the possession of reasonable alternatives. A consumer, for example, really does not enjoy economic freedom as a consumer if there is only one feasible source of supply. To give him freedom as a consumer means that he must be able to choose between several alternatives. Whatever may be said for the technical efficiency of a monopoly, even though state owned and, therefore, presumably operated in the interest of the whole community, it is still true that the economic freedom of consumers is limited by such a single supplier. If that objection exists as to private monopolies, it holds even more clearly for the all-pervasive monopoly which would be represented by a state-controlled economy. In the former case, people would at least have the freedom of choosing between different sellers by directing their purchases to competing things. In the latter case, the same supplier (the state) would be supplying all the things.

Sixth, the necessity for direct state control is reduced, because competition, when it is effectively functioning throughout the whole society, provides a decentralized and impersonal regulation of affairs. The relationship between the existence of competition and the avoidance of state control should always be kept in mind. There are certain necessary economic functions such as the providing of incentives for effort and production, the determination of what products are to be produced and how much and the allocation of society's resources to these different activities; and since an exercise of private power on these points would be intolerable, the preservation of at least a reasonable degree of competition seems to be essential if we are to avoid the alternative of extended power of the state itself. Society cannot tolerate any unlimited sovereign other than the state itself. Hence, if any important group is to be unrestrained by the forces of competition, the logic for state control of it is apparent.

What happens in practice when a genuine decline of competition takes place is indicated by certain periods in which the demand for goods and services of certain kinds is so keen that active rivalry on the part of the suppliers of those services is unnecessary. In the period of very active business, during and immediately following the war, a situation of this kind did to some extent exist. The attitude and services of taxi drivers, waiters, salespeople, service personnel as well as of the larger business units suffered a letdown which impaired their services to the community and which was to be explained by a decline in the day-by-day rivalry for patronage. Incidentally, such an experience suggests a serious problem for a country which strives for full employment; and especially it has a bearing upon the thesis, advanced by Sir William Beveridge, that the ideal condition would be one in which there was continually a larger number of jobs available than there were persons to fill them. In view of the limitations of human nature, it seems inevitable that such a condition would lead to a widespread and continuous deterioration of courtesy, efficiency and productivity. On such grounds it appears that the ideal of full employment presents its own problems just as does the unfortunate condition of widespread unemployment.

It appears that talk about competition representing an unworthy attitude of one trying to get ahead of his fellows, while cooperation is pictured as mutual helpfulness, is quite superficial, at least when applied to economic relationships. Economic competition does indeed imply rivalry; but it is rivalry to serve others. Cooperation, on the other hand, has in practice different implications. It may represent efforts by the members of one group to improve the quality of their services to the rest of the community. This is notably true in several of the professions. The cooperation of the scientific investigators, for example, in the medical field, is commonly directed to assisting one another in advancing the common cause. And in the field of business, the cooperation of cost accountants, market analysts and industrial relations directors may be directed to the improvement of their several arts. In these cases the mutual helpfulness is obviously socially beneficial. But in economic relationships, cooperation may also have a quite different meaning. If the retailers of a town develop a cooperative attitude, they may in their mutual helpfulness decide to close their shops for the lunch hour and on every possible holiday; they may reduce delivery services and possibly eliminate some other practices which are annoying to one another, such as occasional and sporadic price reductions. The mutual helpfulness, in short, may not extend to the consumers. Cooperation in these buyer-seller relationships may in practice be not much different from collusion. Paradoxical as it may seem, therefore, pervasive competition in the field of economic relationships provides the best basis for mutual helpfulness.

The ideal, then, of a free economy is that, as buyers, everyone should have alternative sources of goods and services, and, as sellers, everyone should be limited by the competing offers of others of his own class. Of course, the principle can be stated from the other point of view too: as sellers, everyone should have alternative customers, and, as buyers, they should be limited by the competing bids of others of their own class. This is the essential framework of a free economy. It does not mean that every individual is free to impose his will; obviously, such freedom would restrict the freedom of others. It does mean that the individual has a number of effective alternative choices and that such restraints as exist upon his own freedom of action are imposed by the impersonal forces of the market. It need hardly be said that this, like other ideals, is commonly unattainable in its pure form. An economy, however, which is characterized by these relations and mainly regulated by them deserves to be called a free economy; and when other forces are most characteristic and reliance for the protection of the individuals is placed mainly upon these other forces, the economy is no longer free.

THE PROFIT MOTIVE

—

By Beardsley Ruml *

THE search for profits is probably the most important single motivating force in modern business. Undoubtedly many businessmen experience other impulses in the daily affairs of their business than the sheer desire to make profit: the desire to retain an old and faithful employee whose usefulness is past; the desire to help customers who happen also to be friends by continuing their credit during depression; a genuine feeling of responsibility to serve the public. However, it is still probable that the most widely prevailing motive in modern business is the desire for profits. The following reading describes the profit motive and analyzes its services to the economy.

Profit is the excess of selling price over cost. If a thing cannot be sold, there can be no profit. Nor will there be a profit unless the selling price is greater than the total cost of getting the article into the purchaser's hands.

This familiar relationship between selling prices and costs, which results in profit, causes profit to serve two exceedingly important purposes. In the first place, profits are a test of whether the thing that is made is wanted, and whether enough people want it at the price at which it is offered more than they want something else at some other price. If they do not, there will be insufficient sales and insufficient profits—or none at all.

---

* Beardsley Ruml, 1894–1960, served on the staff of the University of Chicago and was chairman of the Federal Reserve Bank of New York. He was treasurer (1934–45) and chairman (1945–49) of the board of R. H. Macy & Co., Inc. In 1943 he presented the "pay-as-you-go" plan of federal taxation to the United States Senate Finance Committee. As a result, compromise tax legislation was adopted that year which was the beginning of withholding income tax payments from regular salaries and wages.

This selection is from Ruml's *Tomorrow's Business* (1945) and is reprinted by permission of Holt, Rinehart & Winston, Inc., and Mrs. Beardsley Ruml.

In the second place, profits serve as a check on costs, and hence as a means of reducing wastes of all kinds. The costs must be brought below the price at which the thing will sell in adequate quantities, and the lower the cost the greater the profit and the greater the possibility of wider use.

The first purpose that profits serve is to make sure that the thing made is wanted by the people. The necessity of making things which must sell directs the energies of a company into the channels of making things which people want more than they want something else. It stops companies from trying to do things that get no public response and that meet no public need. And since most things compete with other things as objects of human desire, and since they compete both in desirability and in price, the managers of business are forced to seek a right price for the things they have to sell.

The fact that the thing made must be sold if there is to be a profit makes the managers of business attend to other matters than merely *making* things. They must give much attention to the *pricing* of the things they have made and to the *selling* of them. The selling activities of a business are informative services which help to improve the standard of living, and the pricing process is a delicate and admirable device for letting people decide how much they want one thing as compared with something else.

The selling and pricing of things made by business for the use of people sometimes lends to business conduct of a character that the people, through their public government, have made illegal. Misrepresentation in advertising and false branding have been outlawed as a method of getting sales that will yield a profit. So also, most forms of collusion in the setting of prices are considered contrary to public interest and are made illegal "as conspiracy in restraint of trade." The beneficial influences of profit-making in the production and distribution of things for use must be protected by outlawing misrepresentation of the goods sold and collusion in fixing their price.

The second purpose which profits serve is to reduce the cost of production and distribution and, thereby, to eliminate waste of human effort and of natural resources and to make more things available to more people. The beneficial pressure of profit on cost reduction comes from giving an impulse to efficiency and ingenuity; it provides an incentive for the discovery of new processes and new machines for the elimination of waste motion and unneeded services. This kind of cost reduction results in the use of less human effort and less material in the producing and selling of a given article. Economy in the use of our resources of men and materials, while at the same time maintaining the same or a higher standard of living, serves a valuable social purpose, and the pressure for profits is the principal influence to this end.

Just as prices can be fixed and maintained in ways that are unwholesome, so also can the cost of things be cut in ways that are considered unfair and sometimes illegal. The setting of wage rates below minimum standards, pressure for output beyond the limits of health and sanity, adulteration and deterioration of product—these and other methods of cost reduction are at least on the shady side. Profit-making by such means must be checked by public regulation.

Profits, therefore, serve a double purpose: first, they direct the activities of business into channels which meet a public response; second, they provide a pressure for ingenuity and efficiency. Profits are needed for these two purposes, whether the profits, after they are made, are privately owned or not. The ownership of profits is a separate question from that of the usefulness of profits as a directive energizer of business power. An enterprise of the business type, producing goods and services for use, whether it be publicly, privately or cooperatively owned, requires the profit motive and profit statement to make it work and work soundly.

How high can profits properly be? If the goods are sold squarely and priced competitively, if the costs of producing them are governed by intelligence and by the use of fair and legal methods, if there is no direct or indirect public subsidy that makes prices higher or costs lower than the managers of the business themselves could make them, then the higher the profits the better the interests of all are served. A special case exists in the exploitation of privately owned natural resources, where the need of conservation for the benefit of future generations should be a reasonable limiting factor on present profits. But, even in this special case, given a public policy and law as regards conservation, the higher the profits the better.

Unfortunately, public opinion today is skeptical of accepting the highest obtainable profit as a desirable social standard. This skepticism is the result of the practices we have described, which have undermined the prestige of business.

These practices are: improper representation and misbranding in selling; controlled and noncompetitive pricing; exploitation of labor; adulteration of quality; the receipt of subsidies in the form of franchises, tariffs, tax exemptions and grants of the public domain; and, finally, undue monopoly privileges in the use of patents, trademarks and copyrights. When profits are made (1) within the law, (2) under competitive enterprise, (3) without public subsidy, or (4) without public protection of exclusivity, the higher the profits the greater the honor to the profit-maker. Under these circumstances there should be no limitation on the amount of profits which a business can make, because the greater the profits the greater the service.

In many cases, business receives direct or indirect public subsidy or public protection of exclusivity. These privileges are neither unusual nor are they undesirable. The American tradition of public cooperation with private enterprise is one of long standing and it takes many forms adapted to many special situations. These subsidies, protections and immunities, although they have been legally granted, have been excessive in some cases, and they may have been continued over an unnecessarily long period of time. But such errors are errors in the application of principles that need have only pragmatic justification. We need only recognize that where there is public assistance and special privilege there is also the duty of public regulation and the right of public participation in the final resulting profit.

In addition to the two broad social purposes just discussed, profits serve in three necessary ways to safeguard and to promote the safety and welfare of any particular business. In the first place, they are a safeguard against errors in pricing; in the second place they are the foundation on which additional capital can be raised as it is needed; and finally, they are the measuring standard against which the efficiency of the management is tested.

The first reason that profits are necessary for a business is to give a margin of protection against errors in pricing. Goods and services are offered for future delivery at an agreed price which is binding on the seller. The company making the sales estimates what its costs are likely to be. In the case of manufacturing, the selling price can be settled and the uncertainties will occur in the costs of goods to be sold. In the retail business, commitments for the acquiring of merchandise to sell must be made far in advance of the time of sale, and an estimate must be made as to whether at this future date the merchandise will be desirable and whether it will be salable at a predetermined price. In distribution, the costs of goods and expenses can be estimated with fair accuracy, but the selling price and the quantities that can be sold are problematical. In any case, errors in judgment will occasionally be made, and the margin of profit must be sufficient so that over a large number of transactions there is a plus and not a minus resulting from subtracting total costs from total sales.

It follows that the greater the uncertainty of the cost of goods, or of the price at which they can be sold, the larger the margin of profit which must be projected. Efficient management and shrewd forecasting of demand will make profits for some, and under the same circumstances losses will have to be taken by others. But unless the profit differential for the industry as a whole is wide enough to give to the industry as a whole a margin to cover normal human errors in estimating future selling prices and future costs, the position of the industry is untenable. Profits must be large enough to bring risk-taking in pricing and costing within the limits of ordinary business judgment.

The second reason that profits are necessary for a business is to provide a foundation for the raising of additional capital. As a justification for the investment of new capital, profits must be looked at differently, depending on whether the business is an old one with a long operating history or whether it is a new one with its record yet to be made.

Let us consider first an old and established business. Such a business must have profits in order to have access to new capital; it must be able to attract the savings of the people to its operations, when additional capital funds are required. These savings can be brought into the company in any of three ways: (1) as the application of the earnings of the company not distributed to the stockholders; (2) as a loan to the company evidenced by bonds, mortgages or other classes of indebtedness; or (3) by sale by the company of the company's preferred or common stock. In each case, a record of profits is necessary if the company is to get the capital it requires.

In the case of raising capital by the investment of undistributed earnings, the profits must have been made before they can be withheld. Further, no management is justified in withholding earnings which belong to the stockholders unless it believes that the withheld earnings can be used to make increased or surer profits.

If the company decides to raise its new capital by borrowing, the higher the profits have been and the longer and steadier the history of the earnings, the lower will be the cost of capital. Unless a reasonable and satisfactory record of profit-making has been shown, new capital will not be available on any terms. And even when capital is available, the differences in the costs of capital will be significant, depending on the profit-making record of the company. These differences in the costs of new capital are matters of consequence to all parties at interest in the business.

The obtaining of new capital by the sale of stock to old stockholders or to the public nearly always means pricing the new stock somewhat below the existing market price of the stock already outstanding. This market price may be above or it may be below the book value of the stock, that is, of the historic investment which has already been made in the company. Unless the new stock can be sold at or above its book value, the existing stockholders are paying a premium for the new capital. So, unless the profits of a company are sufficient to support a market price that permits the sale of new stock at or above book value, the profits are insufficient to support equal treatment of old stockholders with new ones, and again the position of the company is untenable.

Profits are not the only factor which determines the market values of stock and, therefore, the cost of new capital; but, over the long run, profits are the principal consideration. As a generalization, subject to exceptions in special cases, it may be said that for business as a whole profits as a whole must be considered insufficient unless common stocks as a whole are selling in the market at a price sufficiently above their book value to permit the sale of new stock at book value. If common stocks are selling at a price too low to permit the sale of new stock at book value, access to new capital is too restricted for the health of private business enterprise.

To induce new capital into new business or into an unseasoned business, the expectation of profit must be large indeed. How much return would have to be anticipated to induce the average person to take five thousand dollars out of his savings bank or out of government bonds for risk investment in a *new and untested* business? Would it be 6 percent, or 8 percent, or 10 percent? Obviously, such returns are much too low. Common stocks of standard companies should yield as much as this. Would it be 20 percent, or 25 percent? These rates of profit also are on the lean side. Even at 25 percent after corporate taxes, the business would have to go on earning at this rate for four years in order to return the investment, and at that, the return would be subject to income tax payable by the investor at the rate of his highest bracket. The plain fact is that new equity capital is ordinarily unavailable to new business on a business basis under present conditions. By and large, the possibilities of profits are too low, the tax rate is too high, the period for getting the stake back is too long and the future is too uncertain. Under present conditions, therefore, new business cannot be started on a business basis. A going concern with a good profit record will find abundant capital at reasonable rates, but at reasonable rates it will be loan capital, not capital for the purchase of its common stock.

This is not only a problem for business, it is a problem for statesmanship. If we want new equity capital for new businesses —and even for most old businesses—profit must be higher, tax rates must be lower and the future must be clearer than it has been in the recent past.

Finally, profits serve a necessary business purpose in providing the yardstick of management efficiency. The management of one company is compared with that of another company in terms of the profits it is able to earn in relation to its capital; the management of a company is compared with itself in terms of what it earned a year ago, or with its predecessor management in terms of the earnings of a previous decade; the several divisions and departments of a company are compared each with the other and with standard profit performances within the industry.

Profit as an evaluation of management efficiency is much more significant than mere money or purchasing power. Profit becomes numbers on a score board, the pay-off entry in a competitive game. The incentive to management is not the profit as profit, but the prestige that attaches to having made a good record, to being recognized as being more successful than the management of a competing firm in the same industry, or to having earned more than last year or more than a previous management was able to earn.

For management the profit motive is essentially a competitive motive, which drives where mere love of gain would never drive. The reward to the managers is not primarily the profit, but the prestige symbolized by the profit—success in a competitive game and status among friends and rivals who understand how the score is kept.

Profit as a directive energizer of business deserves more respect than it is sometimes accorded. It would be difficult indeed to find a substitute that would serve the public welfare so well.

THE ECONOMIC NATURE
OF PROFIT AND LOSS

—

*By Ludwig von Mises**

IN the capitalist system of society's economic organization the entrepreneurs determine the course of production. In the performance of this function they are unconditionally and totally subject to the sovereignty of the buying public, the consumers. If they fail to produce in the cheapest and best possible way those commodities which the consumers are asking for most urgently, they suffer losses and are finally eliminated from their entrepreneurial position. Other men who know better how to serve the consumers replace them.

If all people were to anticipate correctly the future state of the market, the entrepreneurs would neither earn any profits nor suffer any losses. They would have to buy the complementary factors of production at prices which would, already at the instant of the purchase, fully reflect the future prices of the products. No room would be left either for profit or for loss. What makes profit emerge is the fact that the entrepreneur who judges the future prices of the products more correctly than other people do buys some or all of the factors of production at prices which, seen from the point of view of the future state of the market, are too low. Thus the total costs of production—including interest on the capital invested—lag behind the prices which the entrepreneur receives for the product. This difference is entrepreneurial profit.

* Ludwig Edler von Mises, economist, received the doctor of law and social science degree from the University of Vienna in 1906. From 1934 to 1940, he was professor of international economic relations at the Graduate Institute of International Studies, Geneva. He came to the United States in 1940, and since 1946 has been at New York University.

Among his books are *Bureaucracy* (1944), *Human Action: A Treatise on Economics* (1949) and *The Ultimate Foundation of Economic Science* (1962).

The following article is from a book of essays entitled *Planning for Freedom* (1962). It is reprinted by permission of the Libertarian Press and the author.

On the other hand, the entrepreneur who misjudges the future prices of the products allows for the factors of production prices which, seen from the point of view of the future state of the market, are too high. His total costs of production exceed the prices at which he can sell the product. This difference is entrepreneurial loss.

Thus profit and loss are generated by success or failure in adjusting the course of production activities to the most urgent demand of the consumers. Once this adjustment is achieved, they disappear. The prices of the complementary factors of production reach a height at which total costs of production coincide with the price of the product. Profit and loss are ever-present features only on account of the fact that ceaseless change in the economic data makes again and again new discrepancies, and consequently the need for new adjustments originate.

Many errors concerning the nature of profit and loss were caused by the practice of applying the term "profit" to the totality of the residual proceeds of an entrepreneur.

Interest on the capital employed is not a component part of profit. The dividends of a corporation are not profit. They are interest on the capital invested plus profit or minus loss.

The market equivalent of work performed by the entrepreneur in the conduct of the enterprise's affairs is entrepreneurial quasi-wages but not profit.

If the enterprise owns a factor on which it can earn monopoly prices, it makes a monopoly gain. If this enterprise is a corporation, such gains increase the dividend. Yet they are not profit proper.

Still more serious are the errors due to the confusion of entrepreneurial activity and technological innovation and improvement.

The maladjustment the removal of which is the essential function of entrepreneurship may often consist in the fact that new technological methods have not yet been utilized to the full extent to which they should be in order to bring about the best possible satisfaction of consumers' demand. But this is not necessarily always the case. Changes in the data, especially in consumers' demand, may require adjustments which have no reference at all to technological innovations and improvements. The entrepreneur who simply increases the production of an article by adding to the existing production facilities a new outfit without any change in the technological method of production is no less an entrepreneur than the man who inaugurates a new way of producing. The business of the entrepreneur is not merely to experiment with new technological methods, but to select from the multitude of technologically feasible methods those which are best fit to supply the public in the cheapest way with the things they are asking for most urgently. Whether a new technological procedure is or is not fit for this purpose is to be provisionally decided by the entrepreneur and will be finally decided by the conduct of the buying public. The question is not whether a new method is to be considered as a more "elegant" solution of a technological problem. It is whether, under the given state of economic data, it is the best possible method of supplying the consumers in the cheapest way.

The activities of the entrepreneur consist in making decisions. He determines for what purpose the factors of production should be employed. Any other acts which an enterpreneur may perform are merely accidental to his entrepreneurial function. It is this that laymen often fail to realize. They confuse the entrepreneurial activities with the conduct of the technological and administrative affairs of a plant. In their eyes not the stockholders, the promoters and speculators, but hired employees are the real entrepreneurs. The former are merely idle parasites who pocket the dividends.

Now nobody ever contended that one could produce without working. But neither is it possible to produce, without capital goods, the previously produced factors of further production. These capital goods are scarce, i.e., they do not suffice for the production of all things which one would like to have produced. Hence the economic problem arises: to employ them in such a way that only those goods should be produced which are fit to satisfy the most urgent demands of the consumers. No good should remain unproduced on account of the fact that the factors required for its production were used—wasted—for the production of another good for which the demand of the public is less intense. To achieve this is under capitalism the function of entrepreneurship that determines the allocation of capital to the various branches of production. Under socialism it would be a function of the state, the social apparatus of coercion and oppression. The problem whether a socialist directorate, lacking any method of economic calculation, could fulfill this function is not to be dealt with in this essay.

There is a simple rule of thumb to tell entrepreneurs from non-entrepreneurs. The enterpreneurs are those on whom the incidence of losses on the capital employed falls. Amateur economists may confuse profits with other kinds of intakes. But it is impossible to fail to recognize losses on the capital employed.

What has been called the democracy of the market manifests itself in the fact that profit-seeking business is unconditionally subject to the supremacy of the buying public.

Non-profit organizations are sovereign unto themselves. They are, within the limits drawn by the amount of capital at their disposal, in a position to defy the wishes of the public.

A special case is that of the conduct of government affairs, the administration of the social apparatus of coercion and oppression, viz., the police power. The objectives of government, the protection of the inviolability of the individuals' lives and health and of their efforts to improve the material conditions of their existence, are indispensable. They benefit all and are the necessary prerequisite of social cooperation and civilization. But they cannot be sold and bought in the way merchandise is sold and bought; they have therefore no price on the market. With regard to them there cannot be any economic calculation. The costs expended for their conduct cannot be confronted with a price received for the product. This state of affairs would make the officers entrusted with the administration of governmental activities irresponsible despots if they were not curbed by the budget system. Under this system the administrators are forced to comply with detailed instructions enjoined upon them by the sovereign, be it a self-appointed autocrat or the whole people acting through elected representatives. To the officers limited funds are assigned which they are bound to spend only for those purposes which the sovereign has ordered. Thus the management of public administration becomes bureaucratic, i.e., dependent on definite detailed rules and regulations.

Bureaucratic management is the only alternative available where there is no profit and loss management.[1]

The consumers by their buying and abstention from buying elect the entrepreneurs in a daily repeated plebiscite, as it were. They determine who should own and who not, and how much each owner should own.

As is the case with all acts of choosing a person—choosing holders of public office, employees, friends or a consort—the decision of the consumers is made on the ground of experience and thus necessarily always refers to the past. There is no experience of the future. The ballot of the market elevates those who in the immediate past have best served the consumers. However, the choice is not unalterable and can daily be corrected. The elected who disappoints the electorate is speedily reduced to the ranks.

Each ballot of the consumers adds only a little to the elected man's sphere of action. To reach the upper levels of entrepreneurship he needs a great number of votes, repeated again and again over a long period of time, a protracted series of successful strokes. He must stand every day a new trial, must submit anew to re-election, as it were.

It is the same with his heirs. They can retain their eminent position only by receiving again and again confirmation on the part of the public. Their office is revocable. If they retain it, it is not on account of the deserts of their predecessor, but on account of their own ability to employ the capital for the best possible satisfaction of the consumers.

The entrepreneurs are neither perfect nor good in any metaphysical sense. They owe their position excusively to the fact that they are better fit for the performance of the functions incumbent upon them than other people are. They earn profit not because they are clever in performing their tasks, but because they are more clever or less clumsy than other people are. They

[1] Cf. von Mises, *Human Action* (New Haven: Yale University Press, 1949), pp. 305–07 and *Bureaucracy* (New Haven: Yale University Press, 1944), pp. 40–73.

are not infallible and often blunder. But they are less liable to error and blunder less than other people do. Nobody has the right to take offense at the errors made by the entrepreneurs in the conduct of affairs and to stress the point that people would have been better supplied if the entrepreneurs had been more skillful and prescient. If the grumbler knew better, why did he not himself fill the gap and seize the opportunity to earn profits? It is easy indeed to display foresight after the event. In retrospect all fools become wise.

A popular chain of reasoning runs this way: The entrepreneur earns profit not only on account of the fact that other people were less successful than he in anticipating correctly the future state of the market. He himself contributed to the emergence of profit by not producing more of the article concerned; but for intentional restriction of output on his part, the supply of this article would have been so ample that the price would have dropped to a point at which no surplus of proceeds over costs of production expended would have emerged. This reasoning is at the bottom of the spurious doctrines of imperfect and monopolistic competition. It was resorted to a short time ago by the American Administration when it blamed the enterprises of the steel industry for the fact that the steel production capacity of the United States was not greater than it really was.

Certainly those engaged in the production of steel are not responsible for the fact that other people did not likewise enter this field of production. The reproach on the part of the authorities would have been sensible if they had conferred on the existing steel corporations the monopoly of steel production. But in the absence of such a privilege, the reprimand given to the operating mills is not more justified than it would be to censure the nation's poets and musicians for the fact that there are not more and better poets and musicians. If somebody is to blame for the fact that the number of people who joined the voluntary civilian defense organization is not larger, then it is not those who have already joined but only those who have not.

That the production of a commodity p is not larger than it really is, is due to the fact that the complementary factors of production required for an expansion were employed for the production of other commodities. To speak of an insufficiency of the supply of p is empty rhetoric if it does not indicate the various products m which were produced in too large quantities with the effect that their production appears now, i.e., after the event, as a waste of scarce factors of production. We may assume that the entrepreneurs who instead of producing additional quantities of p turned to the production of excessive amounts of m, and consequently suffered losses, did not intentionally make their mistake.

Neither did the producers of p intentionally restrict the production of p. Every entrepreneur's capital is limited; he employs it for those projects which, he expects, will, by filling the most urgent demand of the public, yield the highest profit.

An entrepreneur at whose disposal are 100 units of capital employs, for instance, 50 units for the production of p and 50 units for the production of q. If both lines are profitable, it is odd to blame him for not having employed more, e.g., 75 units, for the production of p. He could increase the production of p only by curtailing correspondingly the production of q. But with regard to q the same fault could be found by grumblers. If one blames the entrepreneur for not having produced more p, one must blame him also for not having produced more q. This means: One blames the entrepreneur for the facts that there is a scarcity of the factors of production and that the earth is not a land of Cockaigne.

Perhaps the grumbler will object on the ground that he considers p a vital commodity, much more important than q, and that therefore the production of p should be expanded and that of q restricted. If this is really the meaning of his criticism, he is at variance with the valuations of the consumers. He throws off his mask and shows his dictatorial aspirations. Production should not be directed by the wishes of the public but by his own despotic discretion.

But if our entrepreneur's production of q involves a loss, it is obvious that his fault was poor foresight and not intentional.

Entrance into the ranks of the entrepreneurs in a market society, not sabotaged by the interference of government or other agencies resorting to violence, is open to everybody. Those who know how to take advantage of any business opportunity cropping up will always find the capital required. For the market is always full of capitalists anxious to find the most promising employment for their funds and in search of the ingenious newcomers, in partnership with whom they could execute the most remunerative projects.

People often failed to realize this inherent feature of capitalism because they did not grasp the meaning and the effects of capital scarcity. The task of the entrepreneur is to select from the multitude of technologically feasible projects those which will satisfy the most urgent of the not yet satisfied needs of the public. Those projects for the execution of which the capital supply does not suffice must not be carried out. The market is always crammed with visionaries who want to float such impracticable and unworkable schemes. It is these dreamers who always complain about the blindness of the capitalists who are too stupid to look after their own interests. Of course, the investors often err in the choice of their investments. But these faults consist precisely in the fact that they preferred an unsuitable project to another that would have satisfied more urgent needs of the buying public.

People often err very lamentably in estimating the work of the creative genius. Only a minority of men are appreciative enough to attach the right value to the achievement of poets, artists and thinkers. It may happen that the indifference of his contemporaries makes it impossible for a genius to accomplish what he would have accomplished if his fellow-men had displayed better judgment. The way in which the poet laureate and the philosopher *à la mode* are selected is certainly questionable.

But it is impermissible to question the free market's choice of the entrepreneurs. The consumers' preference for definite articles may be open to condemnation from the point of view of a philosopher's judgment. But judgments of value are necessarily always personal and subjective. The consumer chooses what, as he thinks, satisfies him best. Nobody is called upon to determine what could make another man happier or less unhappy. The popularity of motor cars, television sets and nylon stockings may be criticized from a "higher" point of view. But these are the things that people are asking for. They cast their ballots for those entrepreneurs who offer them this merchandise of the best quality at the cheapest price.

In choosing between various political parties and programs for the commonwealth's social and economic organization most people are uninformed and groping in the dark. The average voter lacks the insight to distinguish between policies suitable to attain the ends he is aiming at and those unsuitable. He is at a loss to examine the long chains of a prioristic reasoning which constitute the philosophy of a comprehensive social program. He may at best form some opinion about the short-run effects of the policies concerned. He is helpless in dealing with the long-run effects. The socialists and communists in principle often assert the infallibility of majority decisions. However, they belie their own words in criticizing parliamentary majorities rejecting their creed, and in denying to the people, under the one-party system, the opportunity to choose between different parties.

But in buying a commodity or abstaining from its purchase there is nothing else involved than the consumer's longing for the best possible satisfaction of his instantaneous wishes. The consumer does not—like the voter in political voting—choose between different means whose effects appear only later. He chooses between things which immediately provide satisfaction. His decision is final.

An entrepreneur earns profit by serving the consumers, the people, as they are and not as they should be according to the fancies of some grumbler or potential dictator.

Profits are never normal. They appear only where there is a maladjustment, a divergence between actual production and production as it should be in order to utilize the available material and mental resources for the best possible satisfaction of the wishes of the public. They are the prize of those who remove this maladjustment; they disappear as soon as the maladjustment is entirely removed. In the imaginary construction of an evenly rotating economy there are no profits. There the sum of the prices of the complementary factors of production, due allowance being made for time preference, coincides with the price of the product.

The greater the preceding maladjustments, the greater the profit earned by their removal. Maladjustments may sometimes be called excessive. But it is inappropriate to apply the epithet "excessive" to profits.

People arrive at the idea of excessive profits by confronting the profit earned with the capital employed in the enterprise and measuring the profit as a percentage of the capital. This method is suggested by the customary procedure applied in partnerships and corporations for the assignment of quotas of the total profit to the individual partners and shareholders. These men have contributed to a different extent to the realization of the project and share in the profits and losses according to the extent of their contribution.

But it is not the capital employed that creates profits and losses. Capital does not "beget profit" as Marx thought. The capital goods as such are dead things that in themselves do not accomplish anything. If they are utilized according to a good idea, profit results. If they are utilized according to a mistaken idea, no profit or losses result. It is the entrepreneurial decision that creates either profit or loss. It is mental acts, the mind of the entrepreneur, from which profits ultimately originate. Profit is a product of the mind, of success in anticipating the future state of the market. It is a spiritual and intellectual phenomenon.

The absurdity of condemning any profits as excessive can easily be shown. An enterprise with a capital of the amount c produced a definite quantity of p which it sold at prices that brought a surplus of proceeds over costs of s and consequently a profit of n percent. If the entrepreneur had been less capable, he would have needed a capital of $2c$ for the production of the same quantity of p. For the sake of argument we may even neglect the fact that this would have necessarily increased costs of production as it would have doubled the interest on the capital employed, and we may assume that s would have remained unchanged. But at any rate s would have been confronted with $2c$ instead of c and thus the profit would have been only $n/2$ percent of the capital employed. The "excessive" profit would have been reduced to a "fair" level. Why? Because the entrepreneur was less efficient and because his lack of efficiency deprived his fellow-men of all the advantages they could have got if an amount c of capital goods had been left available for the production of other merchandise.

In branding profits as excessive and penalizing the efficient entrepreneurs by discriminatory taxation, people are injuring themselves. Taxing profits is tantamount to taxing success in best serving the public. The only goal of all production activities is to employ the factors of production in such a way that they render the highest possible output. The smaller the input required for the production of an article becomes, the more of the scarce factors of production is left for the production of other articles. But the better an entrepreneur succeeds in this regard, the more he is vilified and the more is he soaked by taxation. Increasing costs per unit of output, that is, waste, is praised as a virtue.

The most amazing manifestation of this complete failure to grasp the task of production and the nature and functions of profit and loss is shown in the popular superstition that profit is an addendum to the costs of production, the height of which depends uniquely on the discretion of the seller. It is this belief that guides governments in controlling prices. It is the same belief that has prompted many governments to make arrangements with their contractors according to which the price to be paid for an article delivered is to equal costs of production expended by the seller increased by a definite percentage. The effect was that the purveyor got a surplus the higher, the less he succeeded in avoiding superfluous costs. Contracts of this type enhanced considerably the sums the United States had to expend in the two World Wars. But the bureaucrats, first of all the professors of economics who served in the various war agencies, boasted of their clever handling of the matter.

All people, entrepreneurs as well as non-entrepreneurs, look askance upon any profits earned by other people. Envy is a common weakness of men. People are loath to acknowledge the fact that they themselves could have earned profits if they had displayed the same foresight and judgment the successful businessman did. Their resentment is the more violent, the more they are subconsciously aware of this fact.

There would not be any profits but for the eagerness of the public to acquire the merchandise offered for sale by the successful entrepreneur. But the same people who scramble for these articles vilify the businessman and call his profit ill-got.

The semantic expression of this enviousness is the distinction between earned and unearned income. It permeates the textbooks, the language of the laws and administrative procedure. Thus, for instance, the official Form 201 for the New York State Income Tax Return calls "Earnings" only the compensation received by employees and, by implication, all other income, also that resulting from the exercise of a profession, unearned income. Such is the terminology of a state whose governor is a Republican and whose state assembly has a Republican majority.

Public opinion condones profits only as far as they do not exceed the salary paid to an employee. All surplus is rejected as unfair. The objective of taxation is, under the ability-to-pay principle, to confiscate this surplus.

Now one of the main functions of profits is to shift the control of capital to those who know how to employ it in the best possible way for the satisfaction of the public. The more profits a man earns, the greater his wealth consequently becomes, the more influential does he become in the conduct of business affairs. Profit and loss are the instruments by means of which the consumers pass the direction of production activities into the hands of those who are best fit to serve them. Whatever is undertaken to curtail or to confiscate profits impairs this function. The result of such measures is to loosen the grip the consumers hold over the course of production. The economic machine becomes, from the point of view of the people, less efficient and less responsive.

The jealousy of the common man looks upon the profits of the entrepreneurs as if they were totally used for consumption. A part of them is, of course, consumed. But only those entrepreneurs attain wealth and influence in the realm of business who consume merely a fraction of their proceeds and plough back the much greater part into their enterprises. What makes small business develop into big business is not spending, but saving and capital accumulation.

We call a stationary economy an economy in which the per head quota of the income and wealth of the individuals remains unchanged. In such an economy what the consumers spend more for the purchase of some articles must be equal to what they spend less for other articles. The total amount of the profits earned by one part of the entrepreneurs equals the total amount of losses suffered by other entrepreneurs.

A surplus of the sum of all profits earned in the whole economy above the sum of all losses suffered emerges only in a progressing economy, that is, in an economy in which the per head quota of capital increases. This increment is an effect of saving that adds new capital goods to the quantity already previously available. The increase of capital available creates maladjustments insofar as it brings about a discrepancy between the actual state of production and that state which the additional capital makes possible. Thanks to the emergence of additional capital, certain projects which hitherto could not be executed become feasible. In directing the new capital into those channels in which it satisfies the most urgent among the previously not satisfied wants of the consumers, the entrepreneurs earn profits which are not counterbalanced by the losses of other entrepreneurs.

The enrichment which the additional capital generates goes only in part to those who have created it by saving. The rest goes, by raising the marginal productivity of labor and thereby wage rates, to the earners of wages and salaries and, by raising the prices of definite raw materials and food stuffs, to the owners of land and, finally, to the entrepreneurs who integrate this new capital into the most economical production processes. But while the gain of the wage earners and of the land owners is permanent, the profits of the entrepreneurs disappear once this integration is accomplished. Profits of the entrepreneurs are, as has been mentioned already, a permanent phenomenon only on account of the fact that maladjustments appear daily anew by the elimination of which profits are earned.

A social order based on private control of the means of production cannot work without entrepreneurial action and entrepreneurial profit and, of course, entrepreneurial loss. The elimination of profit, whatever methods may be resorted to for its execution, must transform society into a senseless jumble. It would create poverty for all.

In a socialist system there are neither entrepreneurs nor entrepreneurial profit and loss. The supreme director of the socialist commonwealth would, however, have to strive in the same way after a surplus of proceeds over costs as the entrepreneurs do under capitalism. It is not the task of this essay to deal with socialism. Therefore it is not necessary to stress the point that, not being able to apply any kind of economic calculation, the socialist chief would never know what the costs and what the proceeds of his operations are.

What matters in this context is merely the fact that there is no third system feasible. There cannot be any such thing as a non-socialist system without entrepreneurial profit and loss. The endeavors to eliminate profits from the capitalist system are merely destructive. They disintegrate capitalism without putting anything in its place. It is this that we have in mind in maintaining that they result in chaos.

Men must choose between capitalism and socialism. They cannot avoid this dilemma by resorting to a capitalist system without entrepreneurial profit. Every step toward the elimination of profit is progress on the way toward social disintegration.

ENTERPRISE

—

By D. C. Hague and A. W. Stonier*

ECONOMISTS are agreed that "enterprise" is the special quality which the businessman contributes to his firm, and for which he earnes "profit." The owner of a one-man firm will supply both his capital and his own supervising labor to the firm, as well as providing "enterprise." His total earnings will therefore include payments on all these counts. If one takes his total earnings—what he himself calls net profits—these will comprise, first, a large payment, which represents his "wages of management," and is equal in amount to what he would have received as a salaried manager in a similar firm. The remainder of the businessman's net profits will include a payment for the use of his capital by the firm—a return similar to that which he would have got had he invested his money in securities. If this interest payment, made to the businessman in his role of capitalist, is also deducted from his net profits, the residual amount is "pure" or "economic" profits. These represent a return to the businessman as such. A hired manager could have supplied managerial labor and could have been paid a wage. Similarly, capital could have been borrowed on payment of interest. But the businessman alone can fulfill his one essential function. He alone can provide enterprise; he alone earns profit.

What, then, is this thing called enterprise? What is the essential function of the businessman in the modern economy? Econ-

* Douglas C. Hague, lecturer in political economy at University College, London, is the author of several economics textbooks. He has been professor of economics at the University of Sheffield since 1957.

Alfred W. Stonier, noted author, is senior lecturer in political economy at University College, London.

"Enterprise" is taken from *Essentials of Economics* (1955) and is reprinted by permission of Longmans, Green & Co., Ltd.

omists are agreed that to provide "enterprise" means that one takes what are known as *uninsurable risks*. Every businessman faces many different kinds of risk as he directs his firm in a world where no one can be certain what the future will bring. His plant may be burned down or burgled; he himself may die; a cargo he has paid for may go down in an accident at sea. All these are risks which men have learned to insure against. The modern economy provides insurance companies—themselves run as ordinary profit-making businesses—which allow anyone to insure against theft, death, fire and so on, merely on paying the appropriate premium.

The reason such risks are "insurable" is that an insurance company's statisticians will be able to tell it within close margins of error what is the probability of, say, a man of 40 dying before he reaches the age of 65. They can, similarly, say how likely it is that fire will break out in the firms of clients during any given year. Armed with such knowledge, the insurance company is able to insure people against all these risks on payment of premiums which, since they are spread among all the firm's clients, are quite low. The businessman is only too glad to pay the premium and so avoid the risk; insurance premiums represent a perfectly normal cost of production.

There is, however, one type of business risk which is so patently incalculable that no insurance company will offer to insure against it—except, perhaps, at a prohibitive premium. This is the crucial risk that the businessman may misjudge market conditions so badly that he loses money. This risk is particularly great where the product is new and untried; but it still exists where the product has sold successfully for many years. No one can be certain that even the most successful product will succeed for ever. While it is not usually very difficult to guess what the costs of any product will be in the near future, it is rarely very easy to guess what demand conditions will be like. For example, one year out of ten, bad summer weather may ruin the sales of the clothing trade, but no one can tell when that year will be, or how much money will be lost because of it. It is therefore no accident that businessmen cannot insure against commercial loss. There is no way for even the most brilliant statistician to say how much, if anything, either a given firm or a particular industry will lose in any given year. An insurance company which sets out to insure firms against loss might well go bankrupt itself.

Here then we meet the essential function of the businessman. He is able to earn profits because he takes risks which are not easy to take and which he cannot shift to his workers, his bankers or anyone else. He alone will lose money if he makes wrong decisions about which products to make, how big an output of each to make, what prices to charge and so on. It is because there is always this risk of loss that, on the average, businessmen must earn a certain amount of "pure" profit. Only if they can be sure of doing this will the responsibility of perpetual risk-taking seem worthwhile. A businessman can, after all, sell his firm, work as a hired manager, avoid taking risks and still earn his "wages" of management.

There will be some exceptions to this general rule. The small shopkeeper, for example, may value independence more than riches. Thus it seems likely that some owners of small shops earn *less* than they could have earned as salaried managers working for, say, a chain store. In other words, their profits are *negative;* they represent a deduction from the wages of management which the storekeeper could have earned as an employee in a different firm. Again, it is thought that in the clothing industry, where there are many Jews who traditionally have a strong desire to be their own masters, such businessmen earn less than they would get as skilled employees in other firms. Here again it seems that businessmen are willing to pay for the privilege of independence; the profits they earn are *negative.*

This, then, is the nature of the "enterprise." The economy must pay "profits" to its businessmen if such enterprise is to be forthcoming. It follows that profits will depend on the supply and demand for "enterprise." Where many people are willing and ready to take business risks, profits will be low: where few people are willing to take the risk of becoming businessmen, high profits will be earned by those who do.

This analysis has been in terms of the profits of the owner of the one-man business. How can we apply the analysis to the joint-stock company which is so typical of the twentieth century? In principle, the answer is a simple one. The risks of "enterprise" are now borne by the ordinary shareholders of the joint-stock firm. It is they who gain if the right decisions are taken; it is they who lose if mistakes are made. Obviously, however, the whole body of ordinary shareholders in a firm cannot themselves make business decisions. They are forced to delegate such decisions to the board of directors and to the company's executives. Thus, the modern joint-stock company is typified by a divorce between ownership and control. The ordinary shareholder is the man who supplies "risk capital" and who receives what profits there are. But the business decisions in his firm are taken by his appointed representatives, the directors of the company.

Part IV

—

THE APPLICATION
OF ECONOMIC KNOWLEDGE

ECONOMIC FREEDOM
VERSUS ORGANIZATION
—

By Henry C. Wallich*

OVER a hundred years ago, Karl Marx announced to an un-
suspecting world that capitalism was doomed. Capitalism, said
the *Manifesto,* would drag the masses deeper and deeper into
misery and would eventually break down under the pressure of
its inconsistencies. Ever since, undisturbed by the evidence,
Marx's disciples have kept repeating that capitalism cannot
work.

In 1917, the system that Marx thought superior was inaugu-
rated in Russia. This set capitalist sages to proving more energetically than ever that communism cannot work. Communism
meanwhile has conquered almost half the population of the
world. Russia, starting practically from scratch, has become the
world's second industrial power. Yet until the Soviets put Sputnik
in orbit, the chorus that the communist system is ineffectual
droned on. We fell into the error of copying our critics, in believing that something cannot be true because we do not like it.

In entering upon our discussion of the relative merits of a
free and a controlled economy, I shall try to stay away from
words like "cannot" and "must." Nor shall I appeal to history for
any binding generalization. History proves that things can happen, not that they must. I shall try to weigh strength and weakness, and in doing so endeavor to give the devil his due, however
little I wish to have to do with him. Economic effectiveness is
one thing and the good life is another.

The Strength of a Free Economy

What makes a free economy? First of all, a free economy is a
decentralized economy. Decentralization means that we have
millions of centers of initiative, instead of only one. It means

---

* The following selection is a chapter from *Cost of Freedom* by Henry C.
Wallich, reprinted by permission of Harper & Bros.

variety that stimulates creative thinking. "Crazy ideas" have a chance that might never survive scrutiny by an entrenched bureaucracy. Decentralization means making the fullest use of our individual capacities.

Next, a free economy relies upon free markets to decide what is to be produced, instead of upon a central authority. The market gives the economy high flexibility, and makes it responsive to consumer wishes. If consumer wishes are to rule—and what else should in a free economy?—the free market offers the best means for the allocation of productive resources.

In the third place, a free economy relies heavily on incentives and competition. It offers to reward each according to his contribution, and it holds out exceptional prizes to the exceptional man. Competition stimulates each to do his utmost.

Decentralization, free markets, incentives and competition are the basic mechanisms of a free economy. The more freedom allowed, one must assume, the more intensive and effective will be the work of these mechanisms. It is noteworthy, therefore, that in practice we rather pointedly refrain from pushing freedom as far as it will go. If we felt that no other system had comparable advantages, that presumably is what we ought to do. We would want an economy consisting mainly of very small units, in order to have as many centers of initiative and sources of ideas as possible. This kind of economy would also give us perfectly competitive free markets and would hold out the unique incentive of everybody being able to become his own boss. Is it only perverseness, or the scheming of selfish interests, that blocks such wholesome extension of freedom?

Of course it is not, and most of us are perfectly satisfied to see economic freedom restrained in some respects. The uses of freedom have their limits. Competing with the principle of decentralization is its opposite, organization, as represented by big business. Big business has always been credited with the special advantages arising from mass production. Today, however, big business also claims pre-eminence in two other respects: research, and the ability to finance large investment expenditures to realize upon its research. Much is made of these advantages of big business in contemporary literature.[1] It is refreshing to hear such

---

[1] David E. Lilienthal, *Big Business: A New Era* (New York: Harper & Bros,

forthright speech on behalf of a sector of the economy that until recently preferred to keep itself under wraps. But we must be alive to its meaning. The claims of big business severely cramp the style of several familiar figures: the independent inventor in his attic or garage, the young man striking out for himself in a free competitive market, the small business man who is often said to be the backbone of the American economy. They are all manifestations of the freedom we extol in a sense in which big business is not. To the extent that we accept the superiority of the big corporation, we agree that there are economic forces more powerful than sheer freedom.

Especially intriguing is big business' claim to superiority in the financing of capital formation. The claim can hardly be denied. Big business has better access to the capital market, and it often can finance its expenditures from undistributed profits. But in driving home its superiority in capital formation, big business touches the Achilles heel of the free and completely decentralized economy. The speed with which capital is accumulated in such an economy is unpredictable. Rapid accumulation is possible, but it is not part of the logic of the system. The decentralized system can promise a strong flow of inventions, and efficiency in the use of resources. These are, as it were, among its built-in features. Up to a point, inventions also probably set in motion forces that generate additional savings. But in the main, the flow of savings is regulated by the tastes of the people in the community. The system merely interprets these tastes through the market. It is not the fault of the system if people decide to consume all of their income, nor can it claim credit if they save a high proportion. It works just as efficiently in one case as in the other.

A high rate of saving and a high rate of technological advance are the joint promoters of economic progress, with technology probably the senior partner of the firm. Since the decentralized system can promise the second, but not the first, it can guarantee some progress, but not necessarily at the fastest rate. In practice we have enjoyed very satisfactory progress, because invention has been accompanied by a high rate of business saving, and because

1952); Adolf A. Berle, Jr., *The 20th Century Capitalist Revolution* (New York: Harcourt, Brace and Co., 1954).

we have been willing to save as consumers. But the consumer is not entirely reliable as a source of savings. Big business, by reminding us of its superior power of capital formation, points up one of the advantages that a more highly organized system enjoys over a more decentralized.

As it stands today, our economic system is a combination of the elements of decentralization and organization. We have not pushed freedom to its ultimate limits, but have taken it, as a good thing should be taken, in moderation. This poses some ticklish questions. We are pretty sure that our system contains the right ingredients, but how about the proportions? If we had to do it over, would we order "the mixture as before"? And supposing, as I do, that we would, why do we like this particular combination of freedom and organization? Is it because we feel that it is the most productive combination? Or do we prefer it because we like freedom for its own sake, and insist on a certain substantial amount of it even though production could be increased by adding more organization to the formula? In other words, is there one optimum formula if we care mostly about production, and another if we care mostly about freedom? If so, which of the two formulas are we using, the productive or the free? If we are closer to the free formula, how much production are we giving up as the price of freedom?

These questions go to the heart of the role of economic freedom in American life. To give an honest answer, we must turn to the fully organized and controlled economy and see what alternatives and possibilities would confront us there. Of course, the issue is not whether socialism is advisable for the United States. As of today, and I hope many tomorrows, it is out of the question. A small modification of the formula, a slightly different combination of freedom and organization, is all that need be contemplated. But the principle of organization is best observed where it flowers in its purest form.

OUR ARGUMENT WITH SOCIALISM

For many years, almost everybody in America was sure of one fact about socialism—it didn't work. If ever there was a case where it was not safe to be sure, this was it. Russia had demonstrated to us repeatedly that to say that something cannot work or cannot be done is not a promising gambit in a progressive world. At the beginning of the Second World War, it was widely said that Russia could not hold out for long. After the War we were sure she could not develop nuclear weapons for many years. It took the launching of Sputnik to convince many former sceptics of the economic and technological potential of the Russian system.

In addition to closing our eyes for too long to Russian accomplishments, we have been guilty also of closing our minds to the menacing power of Marxist doctrine. Those who have said that the philosophy of communism consists in keeping the people in poverty so that poverty may keep them in communism show little perception of the intellectual capacity of their adversary. Communism is a formidable intellectual structure, built by first-rate minds over many decades, with an inner logic and consistency that capitalism might envy. The average American, debating with a Russian the merits of their respective systems, would soon find himself in hot water, unless he were exceptionally nimble. An American economist facing a trained Marxist dialectician might find the going even harder.

Yet in our post-Sputnik awakening, the pendulum may well have swung too far. Some of us today seem overimpressed with the achievement of the Russians to the point of believing that everything is possible to them, that they can do nothing wrong —in short, that every Russian is seven feet tall. The obvious fact that we want to keep in perspective is that their system has its considerable elements of strength, and also its considerable elements of weakness. We shall have occasion to note both as we pass muster on the principal objections that have been raised in the West to the extreme forms of economic organization that go by the name of socialism or communism.

The economist's argument with socialism proceeds on a somewhat abstract but quite straightforward plane. Some have argued that it is bound to be grossly inefficient in the use of resources. Others concede that it may have certain short-run advantages but believe that it would tend to stagnate in the long run. A widely held view says that a socialist economy is bound to be authoritarian, militaristic and hostile to the needs of the consumer. Let us take these points one by one.

Is Socialism Necessarily Inefficient?

The view that a socialist economy is bound to be grossly inefficient usually refers to the absence of free markets and free prices. In the absence of free price movements serving as indicators of demand and supply, how are the planners to know what is wanted and how it should be produced? In the absence of a market mechanism that adjusts wages and interest to the productivity of labor and capital, how are the planners to know how much of each to use? In a market economy, there will be a price on capital and on labor, in accordance with their respective productivity and with the demand for and supply of each throughout the economy. Total demand will absorb total supply.

In a socialist economy, wages and interest presumably are fixed arbitrarily, if interest is calculated at all. Suppose the planners now proceed, as businessmen would, to plan production by using the cheapest combination of labor and capital. If labor is relatively cheap, they plan to use more labor, and vice versa. But with prices of labor and capital fixed arbitrarily, the planners will probably find that they planned to use more labor than is available while available capital remains unused, or the reverse. To find the wage rates and the interest rates that will allow both factors of production to be used to the full is impossible without a free market. So runs the argument.

The difficulty is real, but it need not be overwhelming. Even in our economy the market works far from perfectly, yet we seem to manage fairly well. And in a socialist economy, as has been shown by numerous students of this obstruse problem, the price-setting function of the market can be approximated in one way or another. Modern computing equipment no doubt would facilitate such calculations. There is a question, of course, whether a socialist economy will in fact proceed in this way and revise its prices frequently or whether it will increasingly let itself drift into a rigid pattern of unrealistic pricing. The possibility of rational use of resources, at any rate, can hardly be denied.

On top of this basic difficulty, it is observed, a socialist economy must face a host of more practical problems. A huge bureaucracy, extreme centralization, loss of individual initiative, loss of incentives are among the most obvious. How real these difficulties are is demonstrated by the Russians' efforts to decentralize their operations. The aggressive use of incentives, in conflict with the communist objective of income according to needs, testifies to the same effect. Very probably these difficulties are a major drag upon any socialist economy. But quite possibly they can be mitigated, or compensated by advantages in other directions. One is hardly justified in asserting, on the basis of such cogitations, that a socialist economy "cannot work."

Must a Centralized Economy Stagnate?

The second objection, on grounds of long-run stagnation, makes a subtler case, besides having the virtue, for the prognosticator, of not being susceptible of immediate verification. Bureaucracies, it is argued, tend to be static and self-perpetuating, unwilling to tolerate outsiders, and constitutionally disinclined to experiment. Omnipotent bureaucracy runs the risk of choking off original thought. When bureaucracy does innovate, it is sorely tempted to ease the repercussions upon sectors that stand to be hurt, in the familiar fashion of the welfare state. The economy will gradually tie itself up in a web of restrictive, protective arrangements. Progress will come to a halt.

This is an interesting and plausible speculation. It is challenged, but not necessarily disproved, by the speed of the Russian advance in science and technology, and by their complete ruthlessness in dealing with groups that stood in the way of what they considered progress. The Russian bureaucracy has not yet had time to mellow and ossify. And it has enjoyed the tremendous advantage of being able to borrow ideas and techniques from abroad.

Yet one cannot help wondering when one learns about the massive resources that the Russians are investing in research, and the serried ranks of newly trained engineers that they send into their factories. This is not the stuff of which stagnation is made. And though party-line discipline may curb ideas, it need not interfere with the routine of progress, the "habit of innovation" that can be acquired. All one can say of the stagnation thesis is: There may be truth in it, there may even quite likely be truth in it, but there need not be enough truth to turn the scales.

Must the Centralized Economy Be Militarist and Hostile to the Consumer?

A third group of objections culminates in the assertion that a socialist economy must become authoritarian, militaristic and hostile to consumer interests. I shall postpone momentarily the first of these points, the alleged inevitability of dictatorship. It is by far the most important contention and requires a careful look. Let us suppose for a moment that we are in fact speaking of a dictatorship. That kind of system has historically often been predisposed toward the other two—militarism and hostility to consumer interests. The various elements in the picture all re-enforce one another. It usually suits a dictatorship to whip the people into line by dressing up alleged enemies abroad. The appearance of these foreign enemies then makes it necessary to concentrate on armaments and heavy industry. Concentration on armaments and heavy industry is convenient, in turn, because that kind of production lends itself more readily to planning than does a more differentiated output for consumption, while planning errors that occur can be concealed more successfully. Finally, sitting on the consumer also serves the useful purpose of keeping him from getting soft and from demanding leisure that he might misuse to think deviationist thoughts.

Small dictatorships may find the military posture unconvincing nowadays. But there are other means of withholding the economy's surplus from the consumer. Monumental buildings, roads, multiplication of long-run projects and conspicuous investment of all sorts commend themselves. So long as the state and its leaders are exalted at the expense of the citizen, an arrangement competent dictators usually find convenient, the consumer will be shortchanged. Something like an iron law of exploitation seems to weigh upon societies that have lost their freedom: if they are not exploited for one purpose, they will be for another, but exploited they always will be.

This chain of argument is plausible, and richly illustrated by contemporary experience. But not all of its links hold equally well. Consumers have, after all, enjoyed a considerable measure of progress in the Iron Curtain countries. In Hitler's Germany, mass living standards in 1938–1939 probably exceeded the best years of the Weimar Republic and of Imperial Germany, despite the priority of guns over butter.

The repression of the consumer assumed to be typical of this kind of economy signifies something else. The less there is of his, the more there is of the state's. If the state employs these resources productively, it can speed up the rate of progress beyond what could be done through investment from voluntary savings. Part of the forced savings may of course end up in late model military hardware that will soon join earlier models on the scrap heap. But even the most entrenched militarists know that they need an economic base. Investment in steel, oil and other basic industries will therefore be pushed even by a militarist regime. If militarism is only a sideline, the capital goods industries can be expanded further to produce more equipment to expand the capital goods industries still further to produce still more equipment—and so on.

The wartime experience of the United States is a case in point. We are ourselves on record, as regards the effectiveness of a dictatorial system, with actions that speak louder than many words—the nation's actions in two world wars. When the pressure was on, there never existed any doubt what had to be done; the United States shifted from a free system to controls. Patriotism made Americans willing to tolerate the severe repression of consumption that went with this system. There was no opportunity to discover what would have happened if the wartime system had been perpetuated, fortunately. But while it lasted, it delivered the goods.

Forced draft methods like these may build up an industrial structure in ten years that would take twenty-five years by voluntary means. If at the end of some reasonable period production is switched to consumer goods, the consumer may even feel that the horse cure was worthwhile. Most of the totalitarian economies promise that this switch will be made at an opportune moment. None, so far as I know, has as yet found the moment opportune. One can understand that it would rather go against their grain and suspects that they would run into great political as well as economic difficulties if they tried. But meanwhile the capacities of some of these economies are growing at an impressive and alarming rate.

Democratic Socialism—The Worst of Two Worlds?

The rapid growth potential of the centrally controlled economy hinges on one condition: the use of force. A centralized system that is undemocratic, dictatorial and relies on force against its own people has two great advantages. It can extort more savings, and it need not worry about how to arrive at and execute a general plan that is acceptable to a majority. A centralized economy run on democratic lines will have to shift into a very different key.

Democratic socialism can accumulate capital to the extent that the citizens allow resources to be diverted from current consumption. The citizens may wish the government to invest much or little, but in any case they will very probably yield up less than could be invested were the government prepared to override and repress their consumption urges. This is the first problem of democratic socialism and of any form of democratic centralization.

Contemporary experience shows that a democratic country with a highly centralized economy can invest a good deal—witness the much cited case of Norway. But Norway is a small country operating under perhaps exceptional conditions. The experience of other countries that have gone in for some degree of planning during shorter or longer periods suggests that consumers may make demands upon their government that leave inadequate amounts for investment. The adequacy of capital formation in a democratically planned country rates a large question mark.

It is true that big corporations owned by the government—railroads and utilities, for instance—might use their power for the purpose of forming capital just as big privately owned corporations do now. In practice, however, nationalized industries seem to have been used more often to subsidize the consumer than to extract forced savings from him. The United States Post Office Department, with its perpetual tendency toward deficits, illustrates this point in our own context. Compared with the dictatorial economy's capacity for massive capital formation, democratic socialism appears weak in this sector. Quite likely it would prove inferior also to a free economy.

The second problem of reconciling democracy and effective central planning—always assuming that the dilemma is not resolved by escape into authoritarianism—will be encountered when the time comes to agree on a plan. A group of competent technicians would no doubt be able to draw up a consistent plan that should work out tolerably well, provided they can be guided by economic considerations alone. But what if they are exposed to all the pressures of a political democracy? In a free economy, the painful decisions are made anonymously—by the market. In a democratically planned economy, somebody must take responsibility for them—unless he can take the line of least resistance and avoid them. The chances are that decisions will be designed, not to achieve the maximum benefit to the whole, but the minimum injury to any one, perhaps with special benefits thrown in for special interest groups. In this dilemma, all pressures combine to avoid readjustments, shore up losing situations with subsidies and generally do things the easier rather than the better way. To overstrain resources would be a permanent temptation. If the political process were of the nature of the American, with unlimited opportunities for amendment of the administration's proposals by the legislature, the "plan" as finally voted might not even be internally consistent.

The special frictions of planning and centralization might to some extent be offset by gains from more intensive organization. But the analogy between the step from small business to big business and from big business to big government misleads. The first step lifts the economy to a new level of productivity. But beyond a size that varies for particular industries, increases in the scale of mass production fail to pay off noticeably. We have no clear indication that the step to big government would create productivity gains that would make up for the handicaps of democratic planning.

Democratic planning probably would score high in maintaining economic stability. Though changes in tastes and techniques are bound to bring some fluctuations, these ought not to de-

velop into cumulative depressions. Employment, whether productive or not, should usually be full if the planners make that
their principal goal. Not so long ago we might have rated the
capacity to avoid depressions a major advantage of a planned
over a free economy. After the experience of the last fifteen
years, we may perhaps allow ourselves to think that the difference on this score need not be very great.

THE OUTCOME OF THE DEBATE

I have tried to present a view of the relative merits of three
economic systems: the free economy as we have it (with considerable admixture of government) in the United States, the
dictatorial centralized economy typified by Russia, and the
democratic centralized economy, which was approached, although
perhaps remotely, by some European countries in the years
following World War II. In comparison with the free economy,
the Russian system shows elements of decided strength. Its power
to extort savings from the consumer and to carry out plans without opposition gives it an advantage that may overcome grave
handicaps in other respects. If we reject this system, as we most
decidedly do, we must found our rejection on our attachment
to freedom, not on economic grounds. To argue otherwise can
only confuse our own thinking. Good causes are hurt by bad
arguments. And as between reasons based on belief in freedom,
and reasons based on economics, the appeal to freedom strikes
me as the more attractive. We want freedom, and we are willing
to pay an economic price for it, by sacrificing the larger output
that we might have in a forced-draft economy.

As we look at our own free economy, we must draw a similar
distinction between our motives rooted in freedom and those
rooted in economics. If we wanted to push freedom to its farthest
limits, we would move toward some kind of Jeffersonian society
of small independent farmers, shopkeepers and artisans. Because
a pastoral society of this sort would make a very ineffective
economy, we are glad to stay with big business. We are willing
to sacrifice some freedom for the sake of economic gain, even
though we draw the line long before we reach anything resem-
bling a centralized economy.

By claiming, as we so often do, that our free economy maximizes everything at once—the enjoyment of freedom itself, present living standards and future progress—we render freedom a poor service. We are implying that we are really making no sacrifice for freedom. We are getting it cheap, almost as a by-product. The truth is otherwise. Freedom has its cost, and it is our good fortune that we are able and willing to pay it.

Then what of the democratic centralized economy? How does it compare with our free system? Properly implemented, it would have its strong points—large-scale organization and good prospects of avoiding major economic fluctuations. On these scores, however, a free economy today can offer close competition. The principal drawbacks might be the need to please everybody, which would turn every economic decision into a political compromise, the tendency to overstrain its resources and especially the difficulty of forming capital in the teeth of a clamorous consumer demand. The democratically controlled centralized economy lacks the power of the ruthless capital formation of the first and the incentives and the unbiased judgment of the market that propel the other. Thus it might find itself outdistanced by both the dictatorial and the free model.

This judgment of the democratically controlled economy seems to be borne out by postwar experience, which has given pause even to previously enthusiastic planners. The course of true planning never seems to have run smoothly. The difficulties encountered by the European countries that went in—quite moderately—for planned economies, the successes of the free economies and the good record of our own economy seem to have raised the stock of free markets. The once-bright promises have begun to pall, and the belief that "planning will make it so" is waning. Today, a quarter-century after the Great Depression, the case for a free economy once more is strong.

NATIONAL PURPOSES
AND THE STRATEGY
OF ECONOMIC POLICY

—

By Raymond J. Saulnier*

MY subject . . . is the strategy of economic policy, but we cannot begin directly with the strictly economic aspect of these questions because we cannot, as I know you will agree, adequately define or design a strategy of economic policy without having in mind to begin with a clear concept of national purpose. By this I mean not merely a concept of what we are seeking to achieve in a strictly economic sense, though this is essential. What we need is a concept of the kind of world, or perhaps I should say the kind of society, in which we want to live. We need, of course, to know all we can about how the economic policies we choose to follow are affecting our national aspirations and may affect them in the future. But to have a value judgment on such matters, to be able to say, that is, whether a given effect is good or bad, a clear understanding of paramount purpose is indispensable.

Yet a concept of national purpose is by no means always explicit in discussions of economic policy. More often than not it is merely taken for granted. Discourse on these matters typically tends to concentrate on narrowly economic objectives, and on short-run measures of economic performance, at that. Especially, it very often fails to take account of the bearing of what we do

* Raymond J. Saulnier, teacher and research economist, received his Ph.D. from Columbia in 1938, and has been a professor there since 1949. In 1946 he was director of the financial research program of the National Bureau of Economic Research and in 1955 was appointed to the President's Council of Economic Advisers; he was made chairman of the latter in 1957. Saulnier is a member of the American Statistical Association, and in 1944 was elected president of the American Finance Association.

His writings include *Costs and Returns on Farm Mortgage Lending* (1949) and *Urban Mortgage Lending by Life Insurance Companies* (1950).

The selection below is from *The Strategy of Economic Policy* (1963); it is reprinted by permission of Fordham University Press.

to achieve our economic objectives on the institutional framework of the world in which we live.

There is a grave danger in this. The danger is that our policy choices will alter the framework of our society in ways we would not deliberately choose. And because, as I shall argue, the institutional framework of our society is basic to the achievement of our national purpose, the inadvertent result of policy may be to frustrate that purpose.

We can be quite sure that our economic policy choices will affect the forms and structure of our society in one way or another; policy choices are rarely altogether neutral in this respect. But we cannot be sure that the impact will conform to our preferences. Certainly we can have little assurance on this critical point unless we are quite clear as to the kind of social organization we prefer, and as clear as we can be as to how it is likely to be affected by the strategy and tactics of our economic policies. This . . . is addressed, accordingly, to the question of national purpose and to the bearing on our success in achieving national purpose of the efforts we make to reach our strictly economic goals.

The clue to our concept of national purpose is not hard to find; it lies in the fact that in our society the central interest is in the individual. Our highest goals are those that have to do with the development and fulfillment of the individual personality, and our paramount national purpose derives from this. To put it simply, our purpose is to provide the greatest possible opportunity for self-directed personal development and fulfillment consistent with the parallel rights of others. We may call this "responsible individualism." Our society's institutional framework, and in particular the framework of its economic institutions, has a crucial bearing on our success in achieving national purpose, so defined. That bearing is expressed in our belief that maximum opportunities for self-directed personal development are afforded in a society in which economic activity is carried out through the institutions of competitive, market-oriented enterprise, based on the institution of private property. And because economic policy affects the institutional framework of our society one way or another, it can make or break our effort to achieve that success.

Although this belief in the essentiality of an enterprise system for the maintenance of free institutions generally is the traditional view of the American people, it is, as we very well know, a point around which much controversy has centered. The most extreme objection to it, expressed in Marxist-Leninist doctrine, claims that the individual finds full opportunity for development only within the framework of essentially collectivist institutions. But the personal development in which we are interested is not development inspired and directed by a centralized, external power, as in the Soviet state. The essence of personal development as we wish it, in a free society, is self-direction.

It may be protested, as it often is, that the individual in our free society is not in fact free from external influences, and it would be an ill-starred venture to undertake completely to rebut this. However, there is no need to do so. It is not necessary to an appreciation of the values inherent in a free society to believe that in such a society the individual makes his decisions in a kind of institutional vacuum. To acknowledge the impact on ourselves of the world around us should not bar us from recognizing that there is maximum opportunity in the atmosphere of a free society based on the concept of responsible individualism, and within the framework of an enterprise economy, to direct one's affairs according to one's own rights. There need be no absence in such a society of arrangements to protect and advance the common interest, and to prevent the exercise of self-interest by one individual or group from unjustly intruding upon and harming the interests of others. The arrangements we have built into our society to provide these protections are far from perfect, to be sure, but they are remarkably good. And we are alert to their deficiencies and on the whole aggressive in our efforts to correct them.

As concerns the Marxist-Leninist protest and its claims, we are nowadays, fortunately, a good bit more discriminating than has been the case in the past. Whatever may be said of the ultimate opportunities for individual development within the collectivist society—and I have grave doubts as to these opportunities—the record shows clearly enough that these societies have made precious little progress to date in providing them, despite the fact that one such system, the Soviet Union, has had nearly half a century in which to do it. All that is necessary to sense the poverty of such opportunity in the collectivist society is to browse for a few minutes at the newsstand of any one of the cities of the Soviet Union. Not that to browse at our own magazine and bookracks is an altogether edifying experience, for it is far from that; but, even so, the comparison is enormously favorable to us.

It is precisely on this matter of the position of the individual in the society and of the individual's freedom that we place most store. It is instructive, for example, that our most deeply felt complaint against the collectivist system is its failure to respect the interest of the individual, as an individual, and its failure to allow opportunity for genuinely self-directed personal development. To remind ourselves of this reaction to the collectivist system should help to clarify our own concept of national purpose. It should strengthen our dedication to democratic ideals to realize that our fondest hope for the collectivist world is that it will in some manner, at some time, provide the scope and opportunities for self-directed personal development afforded by the democratic, individualistic society.

The ultimate test to which we put the collectivist system runs in terms of the scope of individual liberty which it can provide. Equally, this must be the ultimate and continuing test of our own society. And, thus, a strategy of economic policy acceptable to us must be one that promotes and strengthens free institutions.

On this understanding of national purpose, and on this understanding of how our economic institutions bear on our chances of achieving national purpose, let us consider more closely the character of our strictly economic objectives.

Clearly, our economy and our economic life contribute to national purpose not just by being an open system in which there are maximum opportunities for personal development, but also by helping to maximize, through the efficient use of resources, the individual's economic well-being. This is not to say that the economic factor is the only one bearing on man's well-being. Indeed, it is our rejection of such a view that distinguishes us from the materialists. It is merely to say that by providing for the economic facet of man's well-being our economy contributes to the enhancement of welfare in the fullest and broadest sense. And, of course, when we ask how our economy contributes to man's economic well-being the answer must be by performing efficiently in the production of goods and services for consumption, that is, in the production of goods and services that satisfy human needs and desires, including education, medical care, facilities for religious and cultural life, etc., as well as food, clothing, housing and the rest.

How could it be otherwise? The proposition that the purpose of our economy is to produce goods and services for human consumption would seem to be so obvious as to preclude serious debate, and it is not easy to believe that consumption could be understood in anything but this inclusive sense. But apparently not so. Having stated once in the course of congressional hearings that ". . . as I understand an economy its ultimate purpose is to produce more consumer goods . . ." and having stated this in a context that could leave no doubt in the mind of any reasonable and objective listener that this implied consumption in the broadest sense, I have been astonished to see the view repeatedly assailed. Perhaps the most amazing observation on the question, which oddly enough was made by an economist, is that appearing in a recent study which finds in this attribution of primacy to consumption the key to the difference in the economics of our two national parties.[1] This is a remarkable interpretation, considering all that has been said over the years

---

[1] Seymour E. Harris, *The Economics of the Political Parties* (New York: Macmillan, 1962), pp. 342–43. In passages that are absolutely stunning for their lack of objectivity, Professor Harris transforms a stated interest in "consumption" into an interest in nothing but "longer cars with larger fins, bigger refrigerators, more and more gadgets and gimmicks," and into a lack of concern for "adequate provision for resource development, for medical care, for housing, for social welfare."

Arthur M. Schlesinger, Jr. has addressed himself to the same point, employing language somewhat more lurid than that of Professor Harris. In *The Politics of Hope* (Boston: Houghton Mifflin Company, 1963), p. 83, he writes of the "contemporary orgy of consumer goods" and manages to read into the consumption goal a wish "not to produce better people or better schools or better health or better national defense or better opportunities for cultural and spiritual fulfillment—but to produce more gadgets and gimmicks to overwhelm our bodies and distract our minds." He continues, "As against what we self-righteously condemn as the godless materialism of the Communists we seem to have dedicated ourselves to a godly materialism of our own."

on the objectives of economic effort. It warrants asking the question: What could be the purpose of an economy if it is not to produce goods and services for human consumption?

It is true that over a period of time an increase in the output of investment or capital goods may contribute more to the growth of the economy, and certainly to its capacity for future growth, than an equivalent increase in the output of goods for immediate consumption. But growth in itself is not our end-purpose, and ultimately the expansion of capital goods output is useful and desirable to the extent that it is reflected in some way in an improvement in economic well-being. Obviously, any thought that the objective of maximizing the production of goods for consumption precludes an interest in the output of capital goods must be rejected as devoid of any economic sense.

Nor is the consumption-goods objective to be interpreted as precluding an interest in having an adequate provision for national defense. Certainly no one in our tradition would elevate defense to an end in itself, but neither would any responsible citizen sacrifice adequate provision for defense in order to meet current consumption needs. Questions as to what constitutes an adequate allocation of resources to defense are another matter, and are not in any case questions to be decided by an economist. But there can be no contest between the national security and the claims of the consumer. We understand well enough that it is the economist's function to help show how the needs for defense can be met as efficiently as possible and with minimum disturbance to the economy as it performs its continuing function of producing goods and services for consumption.

A quite different complaint against identifying the production of goods and services for consumption as the objective of our economic system is the ancient, but every now and then repeated, protest that such an objective subordinates, if it does not destroy altogether, any interest in improving the quality of our spiritual life. What is threatened, according to this view, is the dedication to liberty and freedom, the spirit of charity and, not the least, the reflective life itself. And to some this is not just a threat but a reality in the United States.

We must reject this view not because it is entirely baseless but because it is not truly and usefully descriptive of our economic situation and because it suggests completely wrong lines of economic policy. Whatever a relative poverty of consumption goods might do for one's dedication to liberty and freedom, or to one's sense of responsibility for his fellow man, and it is not easy for me to believe that it would necessarily enhance them, I think it is true that neither our intellectual nor our artistic development is currently in danger of being corrupted by an undue affluence. No more than a small minority of academicians, at least, face any such threat. Neither does our population generally; there is ample room for the increase and improvement of consumption for the American population before we need have fears of an undue affluence. And to the extent that we face such a peril, our economy provides an easy escape. The better our economy functions in producing goods and services for consumption, the greater the scope for taking consumer satisfactions in the form of leisure. Through our history we have been able increasingly to enjoy the benefits of material prosperity in this manner. Not everyone may use leisure as you and I might most like to see it used, but this is no reason for our not pressing to the full extent of our resources to improve our efficiency in the production of consumer goods and services and in this way to earn the opportunity for an expansion of leisure and, hopefully, for its beneficial use.

One more complaint on the primacy of consumption-goods production should be noted. This is the protest that an excessive amount of our economic resources are devoted to the output of goods for private use and that our provision for social or public consumption is grossly inadequate. It will be recognized as the argument on "private affluence v. public squalor."

Clearly, whatever this argument has to say as to whether it is better to expand public consumption relative to private consumption, or vice versa, it has nothing whatever to say on the question of placing consumption, as such, or on the increase of consumption goods output, in first place, as the objective of our economic effort. Indeed, it is totally irrelevant to this question. The only sense in which the "private affluence v. public squalor" argument might be construed as having some relevance to the question of economic objectives is if we were, by distorting the commonly accepted language of economic discourse, to regard consumption as consisting only of the use of things purchased privately and were to regard those goods and services which we obtain for final consumption through government as not being consumption at all. In this thoroughly eccentric vocabulary we would be a consumer of educational services if we went to a private school but not if we went to a public school; and we would suffer an immediate drop in the output of consumption services if, other things not changing, we were, for example, to shift the facilities for providing commuter transportation from private to public ownership.

Obviously, such a terminology would make it impossible to conduct sensible economic discourse. We can only mean by consumption goods and services those from which we seek satisfaction as final users, whether they are supplied privately or by government. Thus, the "private affluence v. public squalor" argument, while important on other grounds, is wholly irrelevant to the question whether our economic objectives may or may not be properly defined in terms of lifting the output of consumption goods and services.

There is a sense, however, in which the "private affluence v. public squalor" controversy is relevant to the question of national purpose. The relevance derives from the fact that the decisions we make on the question whether public consumption should be expanded relative to private consumption can have far-reaching effects on the institutional framework of our society. I believe that we improve and expand the opportunities which our society provides for self-directed personal development when we give every possible encouragement to private production and consumption. Similarly, I believe that we improve the position of the individual in our society and improve his opportunities for self-directed development when public production and public consumption are limited to those areas in which it is quite clear that the function involved cannot be performed at all through any practicable form of private effort or where it can be clearly demonstrated that it can be performed more efficiently through public than through private effort. This is the principle—traditional in America—that government should do for the individual what the individual cannot do at all for himself or what he cannot do as satisfactorily as government can, and that all else should be reserved for private initiative and private effort. Obviously, this philosophy of government leaves many questions as to the respective roles of public and private effort still debatable. But considering the collateral benefits that accrue in the political and noneconomic spheres of our life when we rely on private initiative rather than on centrally directed government action, I would resolve all such doubts in favor of private initiative. This is the real question involved in the "private affluence v. public squalor" debate. It is not a question of consumption versus something else. In the end, the debate comes down to a question of how much public consumption one prefers relative to how much private consumption.

Thus, without ignoring the needs of the economy for a vigorous rate of investment in capital goods, without sacrifice of an adequate provision for national defense, without stinting in the provision of assistance to others around the world, without fear that we are corrupting ourselves in a materialist philosophy, and without prejudice to the question of private vs. public consumption, we can say that the object of our economic effort is to improve the economic well-being of our people by raising and making increasingly more efficient our capability for the production of goods and services for human consumption. But more than that we can say, also, that precisely because of the nature of our national purpose—to provide maximum opportunities for self-directed personal development—our success in this effort is greatest when we rely to the fullest possible extent on private initiative and private effort.

THE RELATION
BETWEEN ECONOMIC FREEDOM
AND POLITICAL FREEDOM

—

By Milton Friedman[*]

IT is widely believed that politics and economics are separate and largely unconnected; that individual freedom is a political problem and material welfare an economic problem; and that any kind of political arrangements can be combined with any kind of economic arrangements. The chief contemporary manifestation of this idea is the advocacy of "democratic socialism" by many who condemn out of hand the restrictions on individual freedom imposed by "totalitarian socialism" in Russia, and who are persuaded that it is possible for a country to adopt the essential features of Russian economic arrangements and yet to ensure individual freedom through political arrangements. The thesis of this chapter is that such a view is a delusion, that there is an intimate connection between economics and politics, that only certain combinations of political and economic arrangements are possible, and that in particular, a society which is socialist cannot also be democratic, in the sense of guaranteeing individual freedom.

Economic arrangements play a dual role in the promotion of a free society. On the one hand, freedom in economic arrange-

[*] Milton Friedman, economist, obtained his Ph.D. from Columbia University in 1946. He received the John Bates Clark Medal of the American Economic Association in 1951, and from that year until 1953 was a member of the board of editors of the *American Economic Review*. He was a Fulbright lecturer at Cambridge University 1953–54, and a member of the board of editors of *Econometrica* from 1957 to 1960. In 1962 he became the Paul Snowden Russell professor of economics at the University of Chicago. He holds membership in the American Economic Association and is a fellow of the American Statistical Association, the Econometric Society and the Institute of Mathematical Statistics.

His books include *Essays in Positive Economics* (1953) and *A Program for Money Stability* (1960).

The following article is a chapter from *Capitalism and Freedom* (1962), reprinted by permission of the University of Chicago Press.

ments is itself a component of freedom broadly understood, so economic freedom is an end in itself. In the second place, economic freedom is also an indispensable means toward the achievement of political freedom.

The first of these roles of economic freedom needs special emphasis because intellectuals in particular have a strong bias against regarding this aspect of freedom as important. They tend to express contempt for what they regard as material aspects of life, and to regard their own pursuit of allegedly higher values as on a different plane of significance and as deserving of special attention. For most citizens of the country, however, if not for the intellectual, the direct importance of economic freedom is at least comparable in significance to the indirect importance of economic freedom as a means to political freedom.

The citizen of Great Britain who after World War II was not permitted to spend his vacation in the United States because of exchange control was being deprived of an essential freedom no less than the citizen of the United States who was denied the opportunity to spend his vacation in Russia because of his political views. The one was ostensibly an economic limitation on freedom and the other a political limitation, yet there is no essential difference between the two.

The citizen of the United States who is compelled by law to devote something like 10 percent of his income to the purchase of a particular kind of retirement contract, administered by the government, is being deprived of a corresponding part of his personal freedom. How strongly this deprivation may be felt and its closeness to the deprivation of religious freedom, which all would regard as "civil" or "political" rather than "economic," were dramatized by an episode involving a group of farmers of Amish sect. On grounds of principle, this group regarded compulsory federal old-age programs as an infringement of their personal individual freedom and refused to pay taxes or accept benefits. As a result, some of their livestock was sold by auction in order to satisfy claims for social security levies. True, the number of citizens who regard compulsory old-age insurance as a deprivation of freedom may be few, but the believer in freedom has never counted noses.

A citizen of the United States who under the laws of various states is not free to follow the occupation of his own choosing unless he can get a license for it is likewise being deprived of an essential part of his freedom. So is the man who would like to exchange some of his goods with, say, a Swiss for a watch but is prevented from doing so by quota. So also is the Californian who was thrown into jail for selling Alka-Seltzer at a price below that set by the manufacturer under the so-called fair-trade laws. So also is the farmer who cannot grow the amount of wheat he wants. And so on. Clearly, economic freedom, in and of itself, is an extremely important part of total freedom.

Viewed as a means to the end of political freedom, economic arrangements are important because of their effect on the concentration or dispersion of power. The kind of economic organization that provides economic freedom directly, namely, competitive capitalism, also promotes political freedom because it separates economic power from political power and in this way enables the one to offset the other.

Historical evidence speaks with a single voice on the relation between political freedom and a free market. I know of no example in time or place of a society that has been marked by a large measure of political freedom, and that has not also used something comparable to a free market to organize the bulk of economic activity.

Because we live in a largely free society, we tend to forget how limited is the span of time and the part of the globe for which there has ever been anything like political freedom: the typical state of mankind is tyranny, servitude and misery. The nineteenth century and early twentieth century in the Western world stand out as striking exceptions to the general trend of historical development. Political freedom in this instance clearly came along with the free market and the development of capitalist institutions. So also did political freedom in the golden age of Greece and in the early days of the Roman era.

History suggests only that capitalism is a necessary condition for political freedom. Clearly it is not a sufficient condition. Fascist Italy and fascist Spain, Germany at various times in the last seventy years, Japan before World Wars I and II, tzarist Russia in the decades before World War I—are all societies that cannot conceivably be described as politically free. Yet, in each, private enterprise was the dominant form of economic organization. It is therefore clearly possible to have economic arrangements that are fundamentally capitalist and political arrangements that are not free.

Even in those societies, the citizenry had a good deal more freedom than citizens of a modern totalitarian state like Russia or Nazi Germany, in which economic totalitarianism is combined with political totalitarianism. Even in Russia under the tzars, it was possible for some citizens, under some circumstances, to change their jobs without getting permission from political authority because capitalism and the existence of private property provided some check to the centralized power of the state.

The relation between political and economic freedom is complex and by no means unilateral. In the early nineteenth century, Bentham and the Philosophical Radicals were inclined to regard political freedom as a means to economic freedom. They believed that the masses were being hampered by the restrictions that were being imposed upon them, and that if political reform gave the bulk of the people the vote, they would do what was good for them, which was to vote for laissez faire. In retrospect, one cannot say that they were wrong. There was a large measure of political reform that was accompanied by economic reform in the direction of a great deal of laissez faire. An enormous increase in the well-being of the masses followed this change in economic arrangements.

The triumph of Benthamite liberalism in nineteenth-century England was followed by a reaction toward increasing intervention by government in economic affairs. This tendency to collectivism was greatly accelerated, both in England and elsewhere, by the two World Wars. Welfare rather than freedom became the dominant note in democratic countries. Recognizing the implicit threat to individualism, the intellectual descendants of the Philosophical Radicals—Dicey, Mises, Hayek and Simons, to mention only a few—feared that a continued movement toward centralized control of economic activity would prove *The Road to Serfdom,* as Hayek entitled his penetrating analysis of the process. Their emphasis was on economic freedom as a means toward political freedom.

Events since the end of World War II display still a different relation between economic and political freedom. Collectivist economic planning has indeed interfered with individual freedom. At least in some countries, however, the result has not been the suppression of freedom, but the reversal of economic policy. England again provides the most striking example. The turning point was perhaps the "control of engagements" order which, despite great misgivings, the Labour party found it necessary to impose in order to carry out its economic policy. Fully enforced and carried through, the law would have involved centralized allocation of individuals to occupations. This conflicted so sharply with personal liberty that it was enforced in a negligible number of cases, and then repealed after the law had been in effect for only a short period. Its repeal ushered in a decided shift in economic policy, marked by reduced reliance on centralized "plans" and "programs," by the dismantling of many controls, and by increased emphasis on the private market. A similar shift in policy occurred in most other democratic countries.

The proximate explanation of these shifts in policy is the limited success of central planning or its outright failure to achieve stated objectives. However, this failure is itself to be attributed, at least in some measure, to the political implications of central planning and to an unwillingness to follow out its logic when doing so requires trampling roughshod on treasured private rights. It may well be that the shift is only a temporary interruption in the collectivist trend of this century. Even so, it illustrates the close relation between political freedom and economic arrangements.

Historical evidence by itself can never be convincing. Perhaps it was sheer coincidence that the expansion of freedom occurred at the same time as the development of capitalist and market institutions. Why should there be a connection? What are the logical links between economic and political freedom? In discussing these questions we shall consider first the market as a direct component of freedom, and then the indirect relation between market arrangements and political freedom. A by-product will be an outline of the ideal economic arrangements for a free society.

As liberals, we take freedom of the individual, or perhaps the family, as our ultimate goal in judging social arrangements.

Freedom as a value in this sense has to do with the interrelations among people; it has no meaning whatsoever to a Robinson Crusoe on an isolated island (without his Man Friday). Robinson Crusoe on his island is subject to "constraint," he has limited "power" and he has only a limited number of alternatives, but there is no problem of freedom in the sense that is relevant to our discussion. Similarly, in a society freedom has nothing to say about what an individual does with his freedom; it is not an all-embracing ethic. Indeed, a major aim of the liberal is to leave the ethical problem for the individual to wrestle with. The "really" important ethical problems are those that face an individual in a free society—what he should do with his freedom. There are thus two sets of values that a liberal will emphasize— the values that are relevant to relations among people, which is the context in which he assigns first priority to freedom; and the values that are relevant to the individual in the exercise of his freedom, which is the realm of individual ethics and philosophy.

The liberal conceives of men as imperfect beings. He regards the problem of social organization to be as much a negative problem of preventing "bad" people from doing harm as of enabling "good" people to do good; and, of course, "bad" and "good" people may be the same people, depending on who is judging them.

The basic problem of social organization is how to coordinate the economic activities of large numbers of people. Even in relatively backward societies, extensive division of labor and specialization of function is required to make effective use of available resources. In advanced societies, the scale on which coordination is needed, to take full advantage of the opportunities offered by modern science and technology, is enormously greater. Literally millions of people are involved in providing one another with their daily bread, let alone with their yearly automobiles. The challenge to the believer in liberty is to reconcile this widespread interdependence with individual freedom.

Fundamentally, there are only two ways of coordinating the economic activities of millions. One is central direction involving the use of coercion—the technique of the army and the modern totalitarian state. The other is voluntary cooperation of individuals—the technique of the marketplace.

The possibility of coordination through voluntary cooperation rests on the elementary—yet frequently denied—proposition that both parties to an economic transaction benefit from it, *provided the transaction is bilaterally voluntary and informed.*

Exchange can therefore bring about coordination without coercion. A working model of a society organized through voluntary exchange is a *free private enterprise exchange economy*—what we have been calling competitive capitalism.

In its simplest form, such a society consists of a number of independent households—a collection of Robinson Crusoes, as it were. Each household uses the resources it controls to produce goods and services that it exchanges for goods and services produced by other households, on terms mutually acceptable to the two parties to the bargain. It is thereby enabled to satisfy its wants indirectly by producing goods and services for others, rather than directly by producing goods for its own immediate use. The incentive for adopting this indirect route is, of course, the increased product made possible by division of labor and specialization of function. Since the household always has the alternative of producing directly for itself, it need not enter into any exchange unless it benefits from it. Hence, no exchange will take place unless both parties do benefit from it. Cooperation is thereby achieved without coercion.

Specialization of function and division of labor would not go far if the ultimate productive unit were the household. In a modern society, we have gone much farther. We have introduced enterprises which are intermediaries between individuals in their capacities as suppliers of service and as purchasers of goods. And similarly, specialization of function and division of labor could not go very far if we had to continue to rely on the barter of product for product. In consequence, money has been introduced as a means of facilitating exchange, and of enabling the acts of purchase and of sale to be separated into two parts.

Despite the important role of enterprises and of money in our actual economy, and despite the numerous and complex problems they raise, the central characteristic of the market technique of achieving coordination is fully displayed in the simple exchange economy that contains neither enterprises nor money. As in that simple model, so in the complex enterprise and money-exchange economy, cooperation is strictly individual and voluntary *provided:* (a) that enterprises are private, so that the ultimate contracting parties are individuals and (b) that individuals are effectively free to enter or not to enter into any particular exchange, so that every transaction is strictly voluntary.

It is far easier to state these provisos in general terms than to spell them out in detail, or to specify precisely the institutional arrangements most conducive to their maintenance. Indeed, much of technical economic literature is concerned with precisely these questions. The basic requisite is the maintenance of law and order to prevent physical coercion of one individual by another and to enforce contracts voluntarily entered into, thus giving substance to "private." Aside from this, perhaps the most difficult problems arise from monopoly—which inhibits effective freedom by denying individuals alternatives to the particular exchange—and from "neighborhood effects"—effects on third parties for which it is not feasible to charge or recompense them. . . .

So long as effective freedom of exchange is maintained, the central feature of the market organization of economic activity is that it prevents one person from interfering with another in respect of most of his activities. The consumer is protected from coercion by the seller because of the presence of other sellers with whom he can deal. The seller is protected from coercion by the consumer because of other consumers to whom he can sell. The employee is protected from coercion by the employer because of other employers for whom he can work, and so on. And the market does this impersonally and without centralized authority.

Indeed, a major source of objection to a free economy is precisely that it does this task so well. It gives people what they want instead of what a particular group thinks they ought to want. Underlying most arguments against the free market is a lack of belief in freedom itself.

The existence of a free market does not of course eliminate the need for government. On the contrary, government is essential both as a forum for determining the "rules of the game" and as an umpire to interpret and enforce the rules decided on. What the market does is to reduce greatly the range of issues that must be decided through political means, and thereby to minimize the extent to which government need participate directly in the game. The characteristic feature of action through political channels is that it tends to require or enforce substantial conformity. The great advantage of the market, on the other hand, is that it permits wide diversity. It is, in political terms, a system of proportional representation. Each man can vote, as it were, for the color of tie he wants and get it; he does not have to see what color the majority wants and then, if he is in the minority, submit.

It is this feature of the market that we refer to when we say that the market provides economic freedom. But this characteristic also has implications that go far beyond the narrowly economic. Political freedom means the absence of coercion of a man by his fellow men. The fundamental threat to freedom is power to coerce, be it in the hands of a monarch, a dictator, an oligarchy or a momentary majority. The preservation of freedom requires the elimination of such concentration of power to the fullest possible extent and the dispersal and distribution of whatever power cannot be eliminated—a system of checks and balances. By removing the organization of economic activity from the control of political authority, the market eliminates this source of coercive power. It enables economic strength to be a check to political power rather than a reinforcement.

Economic power can be widely dispersed. There is no law of conservation which forces the growth of new centers of economic strength to be at the expense of existing centers. Political power, on the other hand, is more difficult to decentralize. There can be numerous small independent governments. But it is far more difficult to maintain numerous equipotent small centers of political power in a single large government than it is to have numerous centers of economic strength in a single large economy. There can be many millionaires in one large economy. But can there be more than one really outstanding leader, one person on whom the energies and enthusiasms of his countrymen are centered? If the central government gains power, it is likely to be at the expense of local governments. There seems to be something like a fixed total of political power to be distributed. Consequently, if economic power is joined to political power, concentration seems almost inevitable. On the other hand, if economic power is kept in separate hands from political power, it can serve as a check and a counter to political power.

The force of this abstract argument can perhaps best be demonstrated by example. Let us consider first a hypothetical example that may help to bring out the principles involved, and then some actual examples from recent experience that illustrate the way in which the market works to preserve political freedom.

One feature of a free society is surely the freedom of individuals to advocate and propagandize openly for a radical change in the structure of the society—so long as the advocacy is restricted to persuasion and does not include force or other forms of coercion. It is a mark of the political freedom of a capitalist society that men can openly advocate and work for socialism. Equally, political freedom in a socialist society would require that men be free to advocate the introduction of capitalism. How could the freedom to advocate capitalism be preserved and protected in a socialist society?

In order for men to advocate anything, they must in the first place be able to earn a living. This already raises a problem in a socialist society, since all jobs are under the direct control of political authorities. It would take an act of self-denial whose difficulty is underlined by experience in the United States after World War II with the problem of "security" among federal employees, for a socialist government to permit its employees to advocate policies directly contrary to official doctrine.

But let us suppose this act of self-denial to be achieved. For advocacy of capitalism to mean anything, the proponents must be able to finance their cause—to hold public meetings, publish pamphlets, buy radio time, issue newspapers and magazines and so on. How could they raise the funds? There might and probably would be men in the socialist society with large incomes, perhaps even large capital sums in the form of government bonds and the like, but these would of necessity be high public officials. It is possible to conceive of a minor socialist official retaining his job although openly advocating capitalism. It strains credulity to imagine the socialist top brass financing such "subversive" activities.

The only recourse for funds would be to raise small amounts

from a large number of minor officials. But this is no real answer. To tap these sources, many people would already have to be persuaded, and our whole problem is how to initiate and finance a campaign to do so. Radical movements in capitalist societies have never been financed this way. They have typically been supported by a few wealthy individuals who have become persuaded—by a Frederick Vanderbilt Field, or an Anita McCormick Blaine, or a Corliss Lamont, to mention a few names recently prominent, or by a Friedrich Engels, to go farther back. This is a role of inequality of wealth in preserving political freedom that is seldom noted—the role of the patron.

In a capitalist society, it is only necessary to convince a few wealthy people to get funds to launch any idea, however strange, and there are many such persons, many independent foci of support. And, indeed, it is not even necessary to persuade people or financial institutions with available funds of the soundness of the ideas to be propagated. It is only necessary to persuade them that the propagation can be financially successful; that the newspaper or magazine or book or other venture will be profitable. The competitive publisher, for example, cannot afford to publish only writing with which he personally agrees; his touchstone must be the likelihood that the market will be large enough to yield a satisfactory return on his investment.

In this way, the market breaks the vicious circle and makes it possible ultimately to finance such ventures by small amounts from many people without first persuading them. There are no such possibilities in the socialist society; there is only the all-powerful state.

Let us stretch our imagination and suppose that a socialist government is aware of this problem and is composed of people anxious to preserve freedom. Could it provide the funds? Perhaps, but it is difficult to see how. It could establish a bureau for subsidizing subversive propaganda. But how could it choose whom to support? If it gave to all who asked, it would shortly find itself out of funds, for socialism cannot repeal the elementary economic law that a sufficiently high price will call forth a large supply. Make the advocacy of radical causes sufficiently remunerative, and the supply of advocates will be unlimited.

Moreover, freedom to advocate unpopular causes does not require that such advocacy be without cost. On the contrary, no society could be stable if advocacy of radical change were cost-less, much less subsidized. It is entirely appropriate that men make sacrifices to advocate causes in which they deeply believe. Indeed, it is important to preserve freedom only for people who are willing to practice self-denial, for otherwise freedom degenerates into license and irresponsibility. What is essential is that the cost of advocating unpopular causes be tolerable and not prohibitive.

But we are not yet through. In a free market society, it is enough to have the funds. The suppliers of paper are as willing to sell it to the *Daily Worker* as to the *Wall Street Journal*. In a socialist society, it would not be enough to have the funds. The hypothetical supporter of capitalism would have to persuade a government factory making paper to sell to him, the government printing press to print his pamphlets, a government post office to distribute them among the people, a government agency to rent him a hall in which to talk, and so on.

Perhaps there is some way in which one could overcome these difficulties and preserve freedom in a socialist society. One cannot say it is utterly impossible. What is clear, however, is that there are very real difficulties in establishing institutions that will effectively preserve the possibility of dissent. So far as I know, none of the people who have been in favor of socialism and also in favor of freedom have really faced up to this issue, or made even a respectable start at developing the institutional arrangements that would permit freedom under socialism. By contrast, it is clear how a free market capitalist society fosters freedom.

A striking practical example of these abstract principles is the experience of Winston Churchill. From 1933 to the outbreak of World War II, Churchill was not permitted to talk over the British radio, which was, of course, a government monopoly administered by the British Broadcasting Corporation. Here was a leading citizen of his country, a Member of Parliament, a former cabinet minister, a man who was desperately trying by every device possible to persuade his countrymen to take steps to ward off the menace of Hitler's Germany. He was not permitted to talk over the radio to the British people because the BBC was a government monopoly and his position was too "controversial."

Another striking example, reported in the January 26, 1959, issue of *Time,* has to do with the "Blacklist Fadeout." Says the *Time* story,

> The Oscar-awarding ritual is Hollywood's biggest pitch for dignity, but two years ago dignity suffered. When one Robert Rich was announced as top writer for the *The Brave One,* he never stepped forward. Robert Rich was a pseudonym, masking one of about 150 writers . . . blacklisted by the industry since 1947 as suspected Communists or fellow travelers. The case was particularly embarrassing because the Motion Picture Academy had barred any Communist or Fifth Amendment pleader from Oscar competition. Last week both the Communist rule and the mystery of Rich's identity were suddenly rescripted.
>
> Rich turned out to be Dalton (*Johnny Got His Gun*) Trumbo, one of the original "Hollywood Ten" writers who refused to testify at the 1947 hearings on Communism in the movie industry. Said producer Frank King, who had stoutly insisted that Robert Rich was "a young guy in Spain with a beard": "We have an obligation to our stockholders to buy the best script we can. Trumbo brought us *The Brave One* and we bought it." . . .
>
> In effect it was the formal end of the Hollywood blacklist. For barred writers, the informal end came long ago. At least 15% of current Hollywood films are reportedly written by blacklist members. Said Producer King, "There are more ghosts in Hollywood than in Forest Lawn. Every company in town has used the work of blacklisted people. We're just the first to confirm what everybody knows."

One may believe, as I do, that communism would destroy all of our freedoms, one may be opposed to it as firmly and as strongly as possible, and yet, at the same time, also believe that in a free society it is intolerable for a man to be prevented from making voluntary arrangements with others that are mutually attractive because he believes in or is trying to promote communism. His freedom includes his freedom to promote communism. Freedom also, of course, includes the freedom of others not to deal with him under those circumstances. The Hollywood blacklist was an unfree act that destroys freedom because it was a collusive arrangement that used coercive means to prevent voluntary exchanges. It didn't work precisely because the market made it costly for people to preserve the blacklist. The commercial emphasis, the fact that people who are running enterprises have an incentive to make as much money as they can, protected the freedom of the individuals who were blacklisted by providing them with an alternative form of employment, and by giving people an incentive to employ them.

If Hollywood and the movie industry had been government enterprises or if in England it had been a question of employment by the British Broadcasting Corporation it is difficult to believe that the "Hollywood Ten" or their equivalent would have found employment. Equally, it is difficult to believe that under those circumstances, strong proponents of individualism and private enterprise—or indeed strong proponents of any view other than the status quo—would be able to get employment.

Another example of the role of the market in preserving political freedom was revealed in our experience with McCarthyism. Entirely aside from the substantive issues involved, and the merits of the charges made, what protection did individuals, and in particular government employees, have against irresponsible accusations and probings into matters that it went against their conscience to reveal? Their appeal to the Fifth Amendment would have been a hollow mockery without an alternative to government employment.

Their fundamental protection was the existence of a private-market economy in which they could earn a living. Here again, the protection was not absolute. Many potential private employers were, rightly or wrongly, averse to hiring those pilloried. It may well be that there was far less justification for the costs imposed on many of the people involved than for the costs generally imposed on people who advocate unpopular causes. But the important point is that the costs were limited and not prohibitive, as they would have been if government employment had been the only possibility.

It is of interest to note that a disproportionately large fraction of the people involved apparently went into the most competitive sectors of the economy—small business, trade, farming—where the market approaches most closely the ideal free market. No one who buys bread knows whether the wheat from which it is made was grown by a Communist or a Republican, by a constitutionalist or a Fascist, or, for that matter, by a Negro or a white. This illustrates how an impersonal market separates economic activities from political views and protects men from being discriminated against in their economic activities for reasons that are irrelevant to their productivity—whether these reasons are associated with their views or their color.

As this example suggests, the groups in our society that have the most at stake in the preservation and strengthening of competitive capitalism are those minority groups which can most easily become the object of the distrust and enmity of the majority—the Negroes, the Jews, the foreign-born, to mention only the most obvious. Yet, paradoxically enough, the enemies of the free market—the Socialists and Communists—have been recruited in disproportionate measure from these groups. Instead of recognizing that the existence of the market has protected them from the attitudes of their fellow countrymen, they mistakenly attribute the residual discrimination to the market.